THE MIRACLE OF LOVE

Books by CHARLES L. ALLEN

ROADS TO RADIANT LIVING

IN QUEST OF GOD'S POWER

GOD'S PSYCHIATRY

WHEN THE HEART IS HUNGRY

THE TOUCH OF THE MASTER'S HAND

ALL THINGS ARE POSSIBLE THROUGH PRAYER

WHEN YOU LOSE A LOVED ONE

THE TWENTY-THIRD PSALM

TWELVE WAYS TO SOLVE YOUR PROBLEM

HEALING WORDS

THE LIFE OF CHRIST

THE LORD'S PRAYER

PRAYER CHANGES THINGS

THE TEN COMMANDMENTS

THE SERMON ON THE MOUNT

THE BEATITUDES

LIFE MORE ABUNDANT

THE CHARLES L. ALLEN TREASURY

WHEN YOU GRADUATE

THE MIRACLE OF LOVE

THE
MIRACLE
OF
LOVE

CHARLES L. ALLEN

Fleming H. Revell Company
Old Tappan, New Jersey

Scripture quotations in this text are from the *King James Version of the Bible.*
Scripture quotations from 1 Corinthians, Chapter 13, are identified in chapter 8 of this book.

Excerpt from POWER IDEAS FOR A HAPPY FAMILY by Robert H. Schuller, © copyright 1972 by Robert H. Schuller, published by Fleming H. Revell Company, is used by permission.

Excerpt from DEATH OF A SALESMAN by Arthur Miller. Copyright 1949 by Arthur Miller. All rights reserved. Reprinted by permission of The Viking Press, Inc.

Excerpt from RIDE THE WILD HORSES by J. Wallace Hamilton, copyright 1952 by Fleming H. Revell Company, is used by permission.

Excerpt from A FAREWELL TO ARMS by Ernest Hemingway © 1929 by Charles Scribner's Sons, is used by permission.

Excerpt from HORNS AND HALOS IN HUMAN NATURE by J. Wallace Hamilton, copyright 1954 by Fleming H. Revell Company, is used by permission.

Excerpt from THE BIG FISHERMAN by Lloyd C. Douglas, copyright 1952, by Houghton Mifflin Company, is used by permission.

The poem "Who Loves the Rain" by Frances Shaw first appeared in POETRY March, 1914, was copyrighted by The Modern Poetry Association, and is reprinted by permission of the editor of POETRY.

Library of Congress Cataloging in Publication Data

Allen, Charles Livingstone, date
    The miracle of love.

    "First book of Corinthians, chapter thirteen":
p. 89–126.
    1. Love (Theology) I. Bible. N.T. 1 Corinthians
XIII. English. II. Title.
BV4639.A38   218   72–5430
ISBN 0–8007–0543–2

Contents

Thirty-One Days

Love is, as Henry Drummond said, the greatest thing in the world.

I distributed a booklet to the people of the First Methodist Church in Houston containing thirty-one versions of the thirteenth chapter of 1 Corinthians. I asked the people to read one version of this chapter each day for a month. Each Sunday the sermon was on love. Marvelous things happened in the lives of many people during that month. In many people it wrought miracles.

One Corinthians 13 is the clearest, most complete explanation of love that exists in the world. Reading this love chapter in the different words of the thirty-one versions gives one deeper insight into the inspired understanding of St. Paul.

Not only does the reading teach us about love: As we read each day for a month, we find love gripping our minds—our attitudes begin to change—our actions take on new meaning—our lives become fuller and more complete. We discover that, as love becomes our possession, our relationships with other people are easier, we do our work with more purpose, we feel more joy and less discouragement. Many have discovered that love has potent healing power both for mental and physical illness.

Anyone who sincerely fills the mind with love each day for a month, will very likely experience THE MIRACLE OF LOVE.

CHARLES L. ALLEN

THE MIRACLE OF LOVE

1

It's Love Or Nothing

The Bible, like a great mountain range, has certain high peaks. One of those peaks is 1 Corinthians 13. Just the reading of those words is an uplifting, cleansing experience. Countless poets have worked a lifetime to learn the art of putting words together to produce the harmony which St. Paul has achieved in this masterpiece of his, but almost none have accomplished it.

When one's nerves are on edge, or one's spirit is depressed, the reading of this delightful poetry in prose makes one feel that life is worth the living, that there is good to be found.

More than the beauty of expression, however, the greatest of all Christian preachers is concerned about what he is saying. The content is more important than the beauty of the verse. He is speaking to people who are sick—people who are not living—people who can properly say, "I am nothing."

Nothing—what a startling word to apply to a person! *Nothing* —it means not anything, not at all—the opposite of something —of no account—of no value. *Nothing* even means nonexistent.

Who is a *nothing* person? ". . . and have not love, I am nothing."

"Though I speak with the tongues of men. . . ." As a student I studied English, Latin, Greek, and French. Suppose to those four had been added Russian, Chinese, German, Spanish, Italian, and the more than a thousand other languages and dialects of mankind. Suppose I had learned to speak every language perfectly. Then suppose further that I had communication with life beyond this world and could converse with the inhabitants of eternity. With that accomplishment I would say, "I am something."

"And though I have the gift of prophecy. . . ." Suppose God gave to me complete knowledge of all future events. Through the centuries, theologians have argued as to whether or not even God has this power. About the only agreed conclusion reached is that God knows all knowable things, but there is no final agreement as to what is knowable. If I had this awesome knowledge of the future, I would know more than any person who ever lived. I would say, "I am something."

"Understand all mysteries. . . ." In the city where I presently live is one of the world's finest hospitals for the treatment of cancer. I visit patients there frequently. Many have been cured. Many others have died. In spite of the vast research by thousands and thousands of highly-trained specialists, much about cancer still remains a mystery. Suppose I knew all the answers, not only about cancer, but about every other mystery of man? I would know more than all the scientists have been able to learn. I could save the world all the money it will take to land a space ship on Mars and the countless other planets because I would know all that they would find. If I understood all mysteries, then I would say, "I am something."

"And all knowledge. . . ." As I write these words, I see on a shelf in my study an encyclopedia in many large volumes. I refer to these volumes from time to time, but I know I will never read every word in the entire set. Even if I did read every word, I would not retain in my mind all the knowledge in those books. Suppose I knew everything in every encyclopedia. Suppose all the knowledge contained in the world were stored up in my mind. I would say, "I am something."

"And though I have all faith, so that I could remove mountains. . . ." Perhaps St. Paul is referring to Jesus' words, "If ye have faith as a grain of mustard seed, ye shall say unto this mountain, Remove hence to yonder place; and it shall remove: and nothing shall be impossible unto you" (Matthew 17:20). Here Jesus is saying that faith eliminates impossibilities. In this connection I think of Jesus' words, ". . . The things which are impossible with men are possible with God" (Luke 18:27). Suppose I did have the faith Jesus is talking about. I would then have the power of God. Truly, I could then say, "I am something."

Tongues, prophecy, mysteries, knowledge, and faith—as much as all this represents, I could have it all and still be nothing.

"And though I bestow all my goods to feed the poor. . . ." One is reminded of the young man who asked Jesus what he might do to gain eternal life. The reply was that he should keep the commandments. He wanted to know which commandments. So Jesus named some of them: "Thou shalt do no murder, Thou shalt not commit adultery, Thou shalt not steal, Thou shalt not bear false witness, Honor thy father and thy mother: and, Thou shalt love thy neighbor as thyself" (Matthew 19:18,19).

Just the reading of that list makes me hang my head in shame. I stop right now to kneel with a prayer of repentance on my lips. Consider just the one in that list about false witness. We remember how Ananias and his wife, Sapphira, were struck dead for lying. Suppose everybody in the world today who ever told an untruth fell down and died. There would not be an Adam and Eve left to eat an apple.

This young man who was talking with Jesus said, "All these things I have kept from my youth up: what lack I yet?" Jesus knew that he had not kept all these commandments but He did not correct him. The young man was obviously sincere in wanting the good life, and mercifully the Lord let the past be. So Jesus said to him, ". . . go and sell that thou hast, and give to the poor." The young man just could not bring himself to do it. So the end of the story is, ". . . he went away sorrowful" (vs. 21,22).

We appreciate our possessions, and to give up everything we have is something most men just could not do.

"And though I give my body to be burned. . . ." In this connection, I think of certain saints across the centuries who have died at the stake. It takes courage and dedication beyond the capacity of ordinary men to be tied to a stake and allow the fire to be lighted to consume them. It would be a horrible way to die, but we have the record of many who have said, "Light the fire— I will die for my faith."

However, I think that St. Paul had something else in mind. Burning as a means of putting one to death was probably not practiced in the first century. Crucifixion or stoning was the prevalent means. This was a day when slavery was commonly practiced. Just as ranchers brand cattle today, human beings were branded as slaves in that day. The hot iron was applied to their flesh and those men wore that stigma the balance of their lives. "Though I give my body to become a branded slave. . . ." This is sacrifice in its most complete form. Yet—even such a sacrifice is profitless without love. "It profits me nothing."

Today we do not have "branded slaves," but we do brand ourselves as slaves. "I work hard at my job to support my family." "I keep the house, cook, scrub the floors, care for the children." "I have been singing in the choir, or teaching that class, or visiting prospective members every week." We can talk about how we have worked for others and for the Lord. ". . . without love, it profits me nothing."

If love is absent, all these other things are nothing. Without love, "I am nothing."

WHAT IS LOVE?

Actually St. Paul does not define love. I doubt if anybody can. Someone once asked me to define the word *honey*. I studied about it and finally came up with this definition: "Honey is a sweet, syrupy substance manufactured by bees." I realize that is a very inadequate definition. I know I cannot really tell someone what honey is. I can give one some honey and that one can taste it.

Love defies definition, but it can be expressed. St. Paul names the various expressions of love.

PATIENCE

"Love suffereth long"—is patient—endures long—is never tired of waiting. Love waits without murmuring. Love never gives up.

Once I was visiting a dear saint in the church, a fine woman who had lived more than eighty years. Few people came to see her. Her beloved husband had gone to the Father's House some years before. She was very lonely. Her arthritis was so bad that the movement of almost any part of her body was pain. Living for her had now become suffering. As we talked, she said to me, "Why do you suppose God is keeping me here?" I did not know what to answer, so we sat silently together for some moments. Then she began telling me about her son who was living a life far different from her teachings and from God. She thought out loud some of the wrong in her boy. Then she looked at me and said, "God is keeping me here to pray for my boy." Love is never tired of waiting.

Another story comes to mind. Somewhere I read of a son who again and again got into trouble. His father would bail him out until finally he had spent his life's savings. A neighbor said to the father, "If that were my boy, I would forget him." The father replied, "If he were your boy, I would forget him, too, but he is my boy."

Love learns to wait. The Psalmist said, "Yea, though I walk through the valley. . . ." Along the pathway of every life are some valleys. Disappointment, sorrow, illness, loss—these are some of the valleys. There are many more. Love underscores the word *through*. It knows the valley is not the end.

We recall how Jesus was being taken by those soldiers that night in Gethsemane. Simon Peter attacked with his sword, but Jesus told him to put the sword away. The Lord told how He could pray and the Father would give Him twelve legions of angels (Matthew 26:51-53). He could have fought force with force. Instead of force, he chose the slow method of love. He took the way of the cross—love suffereth long.

"For God so loved the world, that he gave his only begotten Son . . ." (John 3:16). This is the method He is always using. During World War II, many were heard to ask, "Why doesn't God kill Hitler?" But God was patient. As we see wrongs in our world, we wonder why God does not act, but love is patient. He never allows little men to make His decisions.

We become bothered by the faults in other people. Some in our own family may be very difficult to live with. We think of fellow workers, certain neighbors, different people in our city. When love is in our hearts, we are patient with those who make life hard for us.

Two short illustrations come to mind which show the advantage of patience. John Wesley's father once asked his wife, "How could you have the patience to tell that blockhead the same thing twenty times over?" "Why," she replied, "if I had told him but nineteen times, I should have lost all my labour."

When Da Vinci was painting his *Last Supper*, he was chided for standing hours before the canvas without making a stroke. He explained: "When I pause the longest, I make the most telling strokes with my brush."

Patience pays.

KINDNESS

". . . and is kind." *Phillips'* translation puts it: ". . . it looks for a way of being constructive." *New World Translation* says, ". . . and obliging." I like the word Wycliff uses—*benyngne* (benign).

I think one of the kindest acts in the story of Jesus happened at Jacob's well. Notice these words: ". . . Jesus therefore, being wearied with his journey, sat thus on the well: and it was about the sixth hour" (John 4:6).

The next verse begins: "There cometh a woman of Samaria to draw water: Jesus saith unto her. . . ."

For a Jewish man to speak to a Samaritan woman was beyond the bounds of decency. Worse, here was a woman whose reputation was quite tarnished. We can be sure she had been called many vile names. She had been snubbed again and again. She knew the meaning of hurt. But Jesus spoke to her. We read that His disciples ". . . marveled that he had talked with the woman" (v. 27). We may be sure they had plenty to say about it behind Jesus' back!

Not only that He spoke is important—also what He said. He did not condemn her for her actions. He did not berate her for her religious failures. He said, "Give me to drink" (v. 7). He allowed her to feel a sense of worth, to maintain some sense of dignity. This is an example of kindness.

Kindness is described as being love in action. It is those things we do. In this connection, we like to think of the well-known words of William Penn. He said, "I expect to pass through life but once. If therefore, there be any kindness I can show, or any good thing I can do to any fellow-being, let me do it now, and not defer or neglect it, as I shall not pass this way again."

Or, as Wordsworth, in "Tintern Abbey," put it:

> That best portion of a good man's life,
> His little, nameless, unremembered acts
> Of kindness and of love.

Only a very few men in American industry have ever been paid a salary of as much as a million dollars a year. One of those men was Charles M. Schwab. It has been said that Andrew Carnegie did not pay Schwab a million dollars a year because he knew more about steel than anyone else knew. In fact, he had a hundred men under him who knew more about steel than he knew. Carnegie paid him a million dollars a year because he knew how to get along with other people. That ability, however, brought Schwab more than just financial gain. It brought him his deepest satisfactions in life.

When Mr. Schwab was past seventy years old, someone brought a nuisance suit against him. He easily won the suit in court, but before leaving the stand, he asked the judge's permission to say a few words. His comment that day is one of the most remarkable statements on kindness that we have recorded anywhere:

> "I'd like to say, here, in a court of law, and speaking as an old man, that nine-tenths of my troubles are traceable to my being kind to others. Look, you young people, if you want to steer away from trouble, be hard-boiled. Be quick with a good loud no to anyone and everyone. If you follow this rule, you'll be seldom molested as you tread life's pathway. Except," and the

great man paused, a grand smile lighting his kindly features, "except—you'll have no friends, you'll be lonely—and you won't have any fun!"

"What is real Good?"
I asked in musing mood.

Order, said the law court;
Knowledge, said the school;
Truth, said the wise man;
Pleasure, said the fool;
Love, said a maiden;
Beauty, said the page;
Freedom, said the dreamer;
Home, said the sage;
Fame, said the soldier;
Equity, the seer,

Spake my heart full sadly,
"The answer is not here."
Then within my bosom
Softly this I heard:
"Each heart holds the secret;
Kindness is the word."

JOHN BOYLE O'REILLY

ENVIETH NOT

"Love envieth not." Is not jealous. Is not possessive.

Here is one sin from which every one of us needs to be saved. There is something of the Prodigal Son's elder brother in all of us. He could love his brother as long as he was in the far country, as long as he was disgraced. But when he saw his father's arms

about that boy, he was jealous. He would rather stay out in the
darkness, than sit inside at the banquet table with his brother who
had the good fortune of being restored.

Envy and jealousy can slip up on the best of people. In his book,
The Greatest of These, Dr. Granville T. Walker recalls Oscar
Wilde's story of how the devil was crossing the Libyan Desert
when he met a number of his people tormenting a holy hermit.
They tried to involve the hermit in sins of the flesh, tempting him
in every way they knew to do, but to no avail. Steadfastly the
sainted man shook off all their suggestions. Finally, after watching
their failure in disgust, the devil whispered to the tempters,
"What you do is too crude. Permit me one moment." Then the
devil whispered to the holy man, "Your brother has just been
made Bishop of Alexandria," and a scowl of malignant jealousy
at once crowded the serene face of the hermit. "That," said the
devil to his imps, "is the sort of thing which I recommend."

A fisherman friend told me that one never needs a top for his
crab basket. If one of the crabs starts to climb up the side of the
basket, the other crabs will reach up and pull it back down. Some
people are a lot like crabs.

The reason love does not envy is because love is a spiritual
quality. Envy is based on materialism. It might be possible to be
envious of some spiritual gift in another person, but it is highly
unlikely. I have never heard of a person who was envious of
another person's goodness; rather would one be envious of another's position or wealth or talents.

In *The Deadly Game* by Will Manson there is a very revealing
conversation:

TRAPP   I've been around, all right. But as far as I can
see, people are about the same wherever you go.

GUSTAVE   You feel that we all have a certain common humanity which is more important than individual
differences?

TRAPP   Well, actually I was thinking in terms of sales technique. When you're trying to sell a piece of merchandise, it doesn't matter if the customer is rich or poor, young or old, male or female—there are three things you always have to make him believe. One: that he is getting the product for a lot less than it's worth. Two: that all the people he looks up to in the world have got one. And three: that his best friends are going to burn with jealousy because he has one.

GUSTAVE   In short, greed, envy, and condescension —these, in your opinion, are the mainsprings of human conduct?

The tragedy is that the road of envy and jealousy fails so completely to satisfy. Arthur Miller wrote a play entitled *Death of a Salesman*. Two friends are talking:

BIFF   Are you content, Hap? You're a success, aren't you. Are you content?

HAPPY   No!

BIFF   Why? You're making money, aren't you?

HAPPY   All I can do now is wait for the merchandise manager to die. And suppose I get to be merchandising manager? He's a good friend of mine, and he just built a terrific estate on Long Island. And he lived there two months and sold it, and now he's building another one. He can't enjoy it once it's finished. And I know that's just what I would do. I don't know what . . . I'm working for. Sometimes I sit in my apartment—all alone. And I think of the rent I'm paying. And it's crazy. But then, it's what I always wanted. My own apartment, a car . . . And still . . . I'm lonely.

Envy and jealousy can never possibly be satisfied. There was a farmer who was miserable because he could not buy the land adjoining his, but he would have to have all the land in all the world to really accomplish that. But love does satisfy because it is not thinking of itself. A person can love who owns nothing and yet feel happy and have a sense of well-being.

Rudyard Kipling, the brilliant English poet, was speaking to a graduating class at McGill University. He advised the graduates not to care too much for money or power or fame; for, he said, "Someday you will meet a man who cares for none of these things . . . and then you will know how poor you are."

HUMILITY

". . . vaunteth not itself, is not puffed up." ". . . Not forward and self-assertive, nor boastful and conceited." ". . . Does not make a vain display of itself, and does not boast." "Love is not proud." "It does not brag." "Love is not out for display." "Love makes no parade." "It is neither anxious to impress nor does it cherish inflated ideas of its own importance." "It does not put on airs." "Love has no high opinion of itself, love has no pride."

Envy and jealousy is one side of the coin. Boasting and conceit is the other side of the same coin. Both desire to be above one's fellow men—one by pulling the other fellow down, the other by pushing one's self above.

Love learns to be humble and humility is learned in different ways. One of life's pathways to humility is through being hurt. In the second act of Dore Schary's *Sunrise at Campobello*, Franklin D. Roosevelt is saying:

Eleanor, I must say this—once to someone. Those first days at Campobello when I started, I had despair —deep, sick despair. It wasn't the pain—there was much more of that later on when they straightened the tendons in my legs. No, not the pain—it was the sense that perhaps I'd never get up again. Like a crab lying on its back. I'd look down at my fingers and exert every thought to get them to move. I'd send down orders to my legs and toes—they didn't obey . . . I turned to my faith, Babs—for strength to endure. I feel I have to go through this fire for some reason. Eleanor, it's a hard way to learn humility—but I've been learning by crawling. I know what it meant—you must learn to crawl before you can walk.

Sometimes life has a way of putting us on our backs in order to force us to look up. It is in looking up that we achieve this virtue of love—humility.

An amateur artist may paint a picture which he thinks is so good that, as he looks over his creation, he can easily become "puffed up." But let that same artist stand for an hour before one of the masterpieces of Hoffman or Rosetti or Muller or Hunt or Da Vinci or Rubens, and then his self-satisfactions melt away and, instead of being boastful and conceited, he finds new inspiration to greater effort.

A budding poet may be very proud of himself because of some verses he has written. He may become very anxious to impress others with his own genius and think of himself as having every right to put on airs. But let that budding poet refer again to Homer or Milton or Dante or Shakespeare or Chaucer or Byron or Scott or Burns or Gray. Then the temptation to vaunt himself easily is overcome.

The musician might feel inclined toward vain display until he hears again the music of Beethoven or Bach or Schubert or Handel.

Similarly, we Christians have a tendency toward thinking of

ourselves more highly than we ought to think. Goodness is one of the graces we quickly and easily appropriate unto ourselves. Self-righteousness likes to parade itself. But when we stand before Martin Luther or St. Francis or Augustine or Loyola or John Wesley or David Livingstone or William Booth or Booker T. Washington—or more especially, when we stand before Him of whom men could say, "Thou art the Christ, the Son of the living God"—then we make no vain display of ourselves.

Thinking along this line, it is easy to see what Phillips Brooks meant when he said, "The true way to be humble . . . is to stand at your real height against some high nature. . . ."

Instead of belittling one, true humility lifts and enlarges one. In a church at Copenhagen there is the famous statue by Thorwaldsen, depicting Christ extending the invitation, "Come unto me." Someone was standing before that statue and was obviously disappointed. Sensing that disappointment, one who was familiar with the statue said to the visitor, "You must go close to it, sir. You must kneel down and look up, if you wish to see Christ's face."

It is impossible to see Christ in any other way. There is a very good reason why we kneel to pray. The very act of kneeling is important.

When love possesses a person, that person has a sense of being one member of the family of God and thinks of all men as precious.

One day, when Toscanini was conducting a rehearsal at the Metropolitan Opera House, a soprano soloist, who was famous and temperamental, objected to the maestro's suggestions. "I am the star of this performance," she exclaimed. "Madame," Toscanini replied quietly, "in this performance there are no stars." In the performance of love, there are no stars.

No one has said it better than the shepherd's boys in Bunyan's *Pilgrim's Progress:*

He that is down need fear no fall,
He that is low, no pride:
He that is humble, ever shall
Have God to be his guide.

GOOD MANNERS

". . . doth not behave itself unseemly." ". . . does not behave unbecomingly." ". . . is never rude." ". . . doth not behave indecently." "Love is not ill-mannered." "Love has good manners." "Love's ways are always fair." ". . . never haughty." —Reading the various versions of this love chapter, we are thankful for the various meanings which are revealed to us.

This is considered one of the minor attributes of love. The more we think about it, however, the larger it grows in importance. John Galsworthy put this expression of love in its proper place of importance when he wrote in *Maid in Waiting*, "All our institutions, religion, marriage, treaties, the law, and the rest, are simply forms of consideration for others necessary to secure consideration for self."

Indeed, the success of people living together, in what we call society, is based in no small measure on such simple things as politeness, tact, and good manners. The words *gentleman* and *lady* denote qualities both of actions and of character which are extremely desirable—yea, even essential for people in association with each other.

Such acts as holding a chair or opening a car door for a lady, saying, *please*, or *thank you*, writing a note of appreciation, observing good table manners, allowing someone to enter a door ahead of you, saying something nice about a person when you introduce him or her, not contradicting someone telling a story, holding a lady's coat, saying how much you enjoyed being with someone, cleanliness of body and of speech—and the list could go on and on—these so-called little things do make a difference in people's lives. Someone has well said:

> Politeness is to do and say,
> The kindest thing in the kindest way.

One of the best stories I have heard along this line came from Rolland W. Schloerb. A man was once impressed by the courtesy of the conductor toward the passengers on a streetcar. After the crowd had thinned out, he spoke to the conductor about it. "Well," the conductor explained, "about five years ago I read in the paper about a man who was included in a will just because he was polite. 'What in the world?' I thought. 'It might happen to me.' So I started treating passengers like people. And it makes me feel so good that now I don't care if I never get a million dollars."

This illustrates one of the main advantages of all the attributes of love—not only does it make for happiness in others, it comes back to bless our own lives.

We have heard the phrase "mind your manners" since we were children. In most instances, people who are reading these words do that, especially when we are in public. Sometimes we forget it, however, when we are in private. It is sad but true that often we are the rudest to the ones we love the most. We all know that we should be at our best in the circle of those whose love means the most to us.

My good friend, Dr. Robert H. Schuller says it well:

> Of first importance—find out the sensitive area in your mate's life. There is something that will offend him that you would never suspect would be offensive. Everybody has his pet peeves. For myself, it was when

my wife neglected to put the cap on the toothpaste tube the first couple of weeks after we were married.

Husbands, find out what about your life bothers your wife most. Wives, find out what about your life bothers your husband most.

Chances are you do not realize what about you is most offensive to your mate. I recently played the marriage game with my wife. I asked her what habit or behavior pattern about my life was most disagreeable to her. I was positive that I knew what her answer would be. I had about three negative factors in my life that I expected her to mention. Instead she named something that I never thought bothered her at all! We turned the game around and played it the other way. And she never guessed what qualities in her life I found most potentially disagreeable.

This is probably due to the fact that we just really never know ourselves as others know us. Play the game. Find out what in your life is most disagreeable to your mate.

Then by all means use your head and know that common decency and good manners would dictate that you correct or neutralize that negative quality promptly and permanently.

It may be some simple little habit. But remember that—

> It's the little things we do
> > And the minor words we say
> That make or break the beauty
> > Of the average passing day.

UNSELFISH

"... seeketh not her own." "... does not insist on its own way." "... does not pursue selfish advantage."

Now we arrive at the very highest expression of love. Our Lord best expressed it when He declared His purpose in life was "not to be ministered unto, but to minister . . ." (Matthew 20:28).

Psychologists speak of the "narcissus complex," which means an extreme self-love. This comes out of a story in Greek mythology. Narcissus, a very handsome young man, one day looked into the quiet waters of a pool and saw the reflection of himself. He completely fell in love with that self-reflection. To some extent, this happens to all of us and, as Oscar Wilde said in *An Ideal Husband*, "To love one's self is the beginning of a lifelong romance."

Love is so strong it can overcome even the instinct of self. There come to all our minds numerous stories of how people have sacrificed in so many ways, even their own lives, because they loved someone more than themselves. One of the best of such stories is recorded by Victor Hugo in *Ninety-Three*.

After the revolution, a French mother was driven from her home with her three children including an infant. She had wandered through the woods and fields for several days. She and her three children had lived on roots and leaves. On the third morning, they had hidden in some bushes on the approach of some soldiers and a sergeant. The sergeant ordered a soldier to find out what was stirring in the bushes; he prodded the mother and her three children out. They were brought to the sergeant's side, and he saw in an instant that they were starving; he gave them a long loaf of brown French bread. The mother took it eagerly, like a famished animal, broke it into two pieces, giving one piece to one child and the other to the second child.

"She has kept none for herself," grumbled the sergeant.

"Because she is not hungry," said a soldier.

"Because she is a mother," said the sergeant.

This is what St. Paul meant when he said, ". . . love does not seek its own."

Love always gives and, (let it be emphasized) love always has something to give. A classic example is the story of Peter and John on their way to church. A crippled beggar was sitting at the temple gate asking for alms. This man had been crippled since birth and had become a professional beggar. One thing he had learned was that church people were the best people from whom to beg. People who worship God are people who give.

As Peter and John approached, the beggar asked them for alms. Peter said, "Silver and gold have I none." He might have prolonged the list of things he did not have. Neither did he have a formal education, nor much social standing in the community. He was a busy man and lacked much time to spare. He could easily have passed the beggar by. But Peter had a loving concern in his heart, so he added, "But such as I have give I thee!" (Acts 3:6). His was the positive mood. There is no power in what one does not have, or cannot do, or does not believe.

Once after Dwight L. Moody had finished a sermon, a man said to him, "Mr. Moody, in your sermon I noted that you made eleven mistakes in grammar." Mr. Moody replied, "Very likely I did. My early education was faulty. I often wish I had received more schooling. But I am using all the grammar I know in the service of Christ."

We all have limitations and we can use our limitations as an excuse not to give. Peter, however, wanted to give and was not looking for an excuse not to. That is the difference love makes. Peter was willing to give what he could in the way he could. Not having money, he thought about his faith and he gave that. He said, "In the name of Jesus Christ of Nazareth rise up and walk" (v. 6).

Then he gave something else: "And he took him by the right hand . . ." (v. 7). He gave him loving fellowship.

There is a story that Ivan S. Turgenev, the Russian writer, met a beggar who asked him for money. "I felt in my pockets," he said, "but there was nothing there. The beggar waited, and his out-stretched hand twitched and trembled slightly. Embarrassed and confused, I seized his dirty hand and pressed it. 'Do not be angry with me, brother,' I said, 'I have nothing with me.' The beggar raised his bloodshot eyes and smiled. 'You called me brother,' he said, 'that was indeed a gift.' "

As a result of Peter's giving, the story ends with the beggar going with them into the temple, ". . . walking, and leaping, and praising God" (v. 8). When love gives it always blesses.

We think of Sister Kenny who was a nurse in the bush country of Australia many years ago. One day she wired the chief surgeon of a hospital about a strange disease which had struck four children. He wired back, INFANTILE PARALYSIS, NO KNOWN CURE, DO BEST YOU CAN. A year later she told this physician, "There were two more cases even worse than the first four, but all six are well now."

"Splendid," said the doctor, "how badly are they crippled?"

"Why, they are not crippled," she replied, "they are entirely normal."

He was delighted, but very much surprised. He asked, "What did you do?"

Her answer was, "I used what I had—water, heat, blankets, and my own hands."

She found the way by giving what she had. "Such as I have I give" is the autobiography of love.

SELF-CONTROL

". . . is not easily provoked." ". . . nor blaze out in passionate anger." "Love . . . is not irritable." "It is not touchy or fretful." ". . . not quick to take offence." "It is not exasperated." The word in the *King James Version* is *provoked*, but as we read other versions, we have that word enlarged on and made clearer.

It is so easy to think of anger as one of the minor sins. Indeed, it is easy to even think of anger as a virtue. We have heard someone say, "I have a temper," as if that is something to be proud of. Every person has a temper, but not every person has learned the art of self-control. What St. Paul is talking about is the fact that love has the power to so master one's emotions that it is always in control.

Jesus told a story about a man who had two sons. One of those sons became a prodigal who ". . . wasted his substance with riotous living" (Luke 15:13). He committed various sins of the flesh, which we have heard condemned again and again. But that boy eventually ended up at his father's table.

It was the other son who was left out in the darkness at the end of the story. He was the one who was lost. Why? This elder brother had many qualities which we admire. He never did many of the bad things his brother did. He was a faithful worker in his father's fields—yet Jesus did not have one kind word for him.

When his prodigal brother returned home, the story says, ". . . he was angry and would not go in . . ." (v. 28). Why was he angry? Simply because he lacked love in his heart. Notice the pronouns in this sentence: ". . . thou never gavest me a kid, that I might make merry with my friends" (v. 29)—*me*—*I*—*my*. In complaining to his father he said, ". . . This thy son . . ." (v. 30). Gently the father tries to correct him with the phrase, ". . . This thy brother . . ." (v. 32), but he would not accept that relationship of love. The alternative was jealous anger. This was the boy who was lost.

Go over the roll of any church and you find names of people who have quit. Some quit out of indifference, but so often you come to names of people who have quit because something upset them. I heard a man explaining why he could not agree with certain positions his pastor took. Some of the things his pastor said in his sermons were quite offensive to this man. But then he added, "I am not going to let any preacher run me out of my church." There is a man whose love for God and his church transcended any irritations or provocations he might have had.

For one who would learn the fine art of self-control, I have four suggestions:

(1) *Determine your most vulnerable point.* I have known people who could endure prolonged pain, yet would go to pieces under a criticism. Impatience is the problem of many. Some cannot stand it, if everything doesn't go his or her way. At this point, we need to consider our prejudices. The list could be extended as to why people get upset, but the important thing is for each of us to determine our own Achilles heel.

(2) *Try to understand other people.* For example, suppose some person is rude to you. It may be a clerk in a store, or someone you work with, or an inconsiderate automobile driver, or one of your neighbors, or one of your children, or your wife or your husband. Instead of becoming irritated or angry, ask the question: "I wonder why that person acts that way?" That question could have various answers. Maybe that person is sick, or has experienced a deep sorrow, or has been mis-

treated by someone else, or any number of reasons. If we know a person, it is much easier to take a loving attitude.

(3) *Try to understand your own emotions.* When you feel yourself getting upset, try to understand why. This can lead to most helpful self-examinations. Epictetus said, "Reckon the days in which you have not been angry. I used to be angry every day; now every other day; then every third and fourth day; and if you miss it so long as thirty days, offer a sacrifice of thanksgiving to God."

Dr. J. Wallace Hamilton, one of the most gifted and beloved ministers America has known, tells a wonderful story in his book, *Ride the Wild Horses.*

As a boy, the gifted Negro tenor, Roland Hayes, heard an old Negro minister preach a sermon on Christ before Pilate. The preacher contrasted two kinds of power confronting each other. Pilate, irked by the silence of Jesus, cried, "Why don't you answer me? Don't you know I have power?" The illiterate old preacher went on to say, "No matter how angry the crowd got, He never said a mumberlin' word, not a word." Years later, at the peak of fame with his golden voice, Roland Hayes stood before a Nazi audience in Berlin's Beethoven Hall. The audience was hostile, ugly, scornful of a Negro daring to sing at the center of Aryan culture. He was greeted with a chorus of Nazi hisses, growing louder and more ominous; for ten minutes Hayes stood there in silence at the piano, resentment swelling up in him like

an irresistible tide. And then he remembered the sermon of long ago: "He never said a mumberlin' word,
not a word." He shouted back no words born in anger;
he kept his head, for he knew that the ultimate power
was on his side, not theirs. He stood there and prayed,
silently, and the quiet dignity of his courage conquered
the savage spirits in his audience, and in hushed pianis-
simo he began to sing a song of Schubert's. He won,
without so much as "a mumberlin' word."

(4) *Develop companionship with God.* I have played
golf with a certain friend many times. I have been told
that on the golf course he easily becomes frustrated and,
after a bad shot, will use loud profanity. In fact, he is
noted for this behavior. Yet, in all the times we have
played together, I have never seen him lose his temper
or express a word of profanity. I asked him about this
one day and he replied, "When I am with my preacher
I control myself."

Suppose one realized that he or she is in God's pres-
ence at all times. What a marvelous difference that
would make! Mrs. Fulton Oursler said that when she
felt herself getting provoked, she would count up to ten.
Then one day she thought of the first ten words of the
Lord's Prayer. Now instead of counting up to ten, she
slowly says, "Our Father which art in heaven, Hallowed
be thy name."

"He that is slow to anger is better than the mighty;
and he that ruleth his spirit than he that taketh a city"
(Proverbs 16:32).

I do not ask for any crown
But that which all may win;
Nor try to conquer any world
Except the one within.
Be Thou my guide until I find
Led by a tender hand,
The happy kingdom in myself
And dare to take command.

LOUISA MAY ALCOTT

FORGIVES AND FORGETS

". . . thinketh no evil." ". . . never resentful." ". . . nor does she reckon up her wrongs." "It never harbors evil thoughts." "It is not touchy." ". . . will hardly even notice when others do us wrong." ". . . does not imagine evil." ". . . does not brood over an injury." Again—it is wonderful how the various translators illuminate the meaning of God's words.

One of life's temptations is to wear our feelings "on our sleeve." In some strange way, getting our feelings hurt ministers to our ego. To forgive or forget a wrong toward us is in a sense to surrender. It is our natural inclination to fight back.

Let me recount here a personal experience which has been real good for me. When I was in the fourth grade in school, the superintendent of that school did me a wrong. I knew it then and I know it now. He fell out with my father about something and he took it out on me. We moved away from that town, and for years I did not see him again.

Then, during my first pastorate out of the seminary, we crossed paths again. This was during a period of depression when jobs were hard to get. If a school board had a vacancy, they received a stack of applications. This man had lost his job the year before and had been trying all the summer to find another place, but without success. Just a few days before school was to begin, the superintendent in the town where I was living resigned. This man applied for that place. I heard about it and I said to myself, "It has been a long time."

I knew that as soon as I told my friends on the school board what I knew about that man—and some other things I thought up about him—they would not hire him. I went out to get in my car to go see some of the board members and suddenly it came over me what I had done. Here I was out trying to represent Him who was nailed to the Cross and me carrying a grudge. That realization was a humiliating experience. I went back into my house, knelt by my bedside and said, "Lord, if you will forgive me of this, I will never be guilty any more." That experience and that promise are among the best things that ever happened in my life.

Love just cannot be sensitive, touchy, unforgiving. A minister tells of a lady in his church who was on a committee. It was announced that a meeting of the committee was to be held in another woman's home who was also on the committee. The lady said to the minister, "After what she did, I will not set foot in her house."

The minister asked when she joined that church. She told him twenty-seven years ago. Then he began to name each one of the ministers who had been at that church during those years. He pointed out that each one was a capable and faithful preacher of the gospel. Then he said, "You mean to say that for twenty-seven years in this church, you have sat here as the love of Christ was preached and now you say you will not 'set foot in her house'?" Then sadly he added, "Lady, what have you heard in church?"

It is so easy to keep account of wrongs against us, to be too sensitive, to look for evil when none was intended. But love almost refuses to be insulted or to be hurt. There is a toughness and a strength about love that protects one's heart and feelings, like a suit of armor protects the body.

IS NOT GLAD BECAUSE OF WRONG

". . . rejoiceth not in iniquity, but rejoiceth in the truth."
". . . never glad when others go wrong." ". . . Takes no pleasure in other people's sins."

Over and over we have heard the saying, "Love is blind." That is not true. Love has eyes that can see and love is aware. But let it be emphasized that love also has eyelids, and sometimes love chooses to close its eyes and not see. Love looks for the good instead of the bad, and when someone does wrong, love is always genuinely regretful.

A friend of mine, who raises turkeys, told me that when a turkey is wounded and gets a spot of blood on its feathers, the other turkeys will peck at that spot until they literally peck the wounded turkey to death. Alas—people can be like that. Here is a place where we must be very careful. It is so easy to be glad when someone goes wrong. The reason is that it ministers to our own' conceits. We have not done that particular wrong and that makes us feel self-righteous.

Gossip is one sin for which restitution cannot be made most of the time. A woman confessed to Philip Neri that she had been spreading slanderous reports. He said, "Go into the market, buy a chicken, pluck out its feathers, and throw them away, and return to me." She obeyed. "Now go back and bring all the feathers you have scattered," said Neri.

"That is impossible," said the woman.

"Yes," said Neri, "your words of slander have been carried about in every direction, and you cannot recall them."

Four reasons come to mind as to why we are glad when others go wrong:

> (1) Being conscious of our own sins, we take comfort
> in the fact that we are not the only ones who have done
> wrong.

(2) Because we are jealous. Sometimes we secretly in our hearts would like to commit the same sins we condemn, but we lack the nerve, or the opportunity, or our own consciences will not let us.

(3) We do not know all the facts about the other person. On the Cross, Jesus prayed, "Father forgive them . . .". Why did He pray that prayer? Because He knew the limitations of their own understanding: ". . . for they know not what they do" (Luke 23:34). If we really knew the other person, we would be much kinder.

(4) Because we lack love in our hearts. I like the story about the father who overheard one of his sons say, "If you do that, Father won't love you." He said to his children, "I shall always love you. When you do what is right, I love you with a glad heart, and when you do what is wrong, I still love you, but with a heart full of sorrow."

James Whitcomb Riley said it beautifully in some verses entitled, "Let Something Good Be Said":

> When over the fair frame of friend or foe
>   The shadow of disgrace shall fall, instead
> Of words of blame, or proof of so and so,
>   Let something good be said.
>
> Forget not that no fellow-being yet
>   May fall so low but love may lift his head;
> Even the cheek of shame with tears is wet,
>   If something good be said.

No generous heart may vainly turn aside
    In ways of sympathy; no soul so dead
But may awaken strong and glorified,
    If something good be said.

And so I charge ye, by the thorny crown,
    And by the cross on which the Saviour bled,
And by your own soul's hope of fair renown,
    Let something good be said.

These words, "Rejoiceth not in iniquity, but rejoiceth in the truth," are well illustrated by the story of Xanthus ordering his servant, Aesop, to provide the best things in the market for his guests. Each course consisted of tongue with different sauces. When Xanthus complained, Aesop said, "Nothing is better than tongue. It is the bond of civil society, the organ of truth and reason, the instrument of our praise of God."

The next day Xanthus ordered the worst things in the market, and Aesop provided tongue. When reprimanded, Aesop said, "The tongue is the worst thing. It is lies, blasphemies, the source of division and war." The tongue can be the worst part of man; or it can be the best part.

This attribute of love is summed up in a story from the first book in the Bible. Let us read it together:

> And Noah began to be an husbandman, and he planted a vineyard: And he drank of the wine, and was drunken; and he was uncovered within his tent. And Ham, the father of Canaan, saw the nakedness of his father, and told his two brethren without. And Shem and Japheth took a garment, and laid it upon both their shoulders, and went backward, and covered the naked-

ness of their father; and their faces were backward, and they saw not their father's nakedness. And Noah awoke from his wine, and knew what his younger son had done unto him. And he said, Cursed be Canaan; a servant of servants shall he be unto his brethren. And he said, Blessed be the Lord God of Shem; and Canaan shall be his servant. God shall enlarge Japheth, and he shall dwell in the tents of Shem; and Canaan shall be his servant.

Genesis 9:20–27

It has always been to the credit of Shem and Japheth that they refused to look upon their father's shame.

SUPPORTING STATEMENTS

In the foregoing phrases we have St. Paul's analysis of love. Then comes a series of strong statements which support and strengthen his exalted view of love.

LOVE WILL ENDURE

". . . Beareth all things, believeth all things, hopeth all things, endureth all things. Love never faileth: but whether there be prophecies, they shall fail; whether there be knowledge, it shall vanish away." —Love is the one thing that will last, no matter what happens and even when everything else is gone.

John Steinbeck said it well in *East of Eden:* "We have only one story. All novels, all poetry, are built on the never-ending contest in ourselves of good and evil. And it occurs to me that evil must constantly respawn, while good, while virtue, is immortal. Vice has always a new fresh young face, while virtue is venerable as nothing else in the world is."

LOVE WAITS FOR THE FULL ANSWER

"For we know in part, and we prophesy in part. But when that
which is perfect is come, then that which is in part shall be done
away . . . For now we see through a glass, darkly: but then face
to face: now I know in part; but then shall I know even as also
I am known."

These words strike a responsive chord in every human heart.
There are so many times when we wonder why certain things
happened. Why sickness—handicaps—disappointment—wrecks
—war—death, and all the others. Sooner or later each of us will
ask, "Why?" and will realize we do ". . . see through a glass
darkly." We just cannot find an answer.

One thing to be said is that life's possibilities come in pairs:
goodness and evil, short and tall, strong and weak, hot and cold
—and also pain and pleasure. The existence of one assures the
possibility of the other. Every possible blessing is also a possible
pain.

Take love out of the human heart and you will also be taking away most of our capacity to be hurt, but that is too high
a price to pay. At times we must resign ourselves to our lack
of understanding, but we find our strength in our faith that
God knows and that God cares. The Psalmist put two wonderful statements together: "He healeth the broken in heart,
and bindeth up their wounds. He telleth the number of stars;
he calleth them all by their names" (Psalm 147:3,4). That is,
the God who watches over all the universe also cares for each
of His children.

There are some things we will not understand but we have the
blessed promise that someday it will all be cleared up for us: "Now
I know in part, but then shall I know. . . ." I quote and I believe
the words:

Not now but in the coming years,
It may be in a better land;
We'll learn the meaning of our tears,
And there, sometime, we'll understand.

MAXWELL N. CORNELIUS

I mention another thought at this point. The fact that "Now we see through a glass, darkly" can be very merciful. We would not want to see clearly the future, even if we could. We are satisfied to live each day as it comes.

LOVE GROWS UP

"When I was a child, I spake as a child, I understood as a child, I thought as a child: but when I became a man, I put away childish things."

Life brings no greater blessing than a child, but it is a heart-breaking tragedy for a child to never develop, physically or mentally. And some people never mature. Let us list several characteristics of little children:

(1) Children become very upset over any personal hurt. If pins prick the flesh, they will cry as if deadly wounded. They are not the most concerned about the suffering of others, they weep mostly for themselves.

(2) Children want to be the center of attention. They are jealous of all about them. They are willing to play, if they can choose the game. They demand applause and appreciation.

(3) Children have to be taught to be thankful. Gratitude for them does not come naturally. They take all the blessings of life as a matter of course.

(4) Children owe nobody anything. Their attitude is

to get all they can but they have little obligation to any person. They rarely think of what they owe their parents or the society in which they live.

(5) Children are completely self-centered. They live in a world that revolves about themselves.

When one grows up (puts away childish things), it does not mean that tears never come to their eyes. It does mean that tears are reserved for causes that deserve them and never given to petty trifles. A mature person can and does weep over his own personal hurts, but more often the tears of love are for the hurts of others.

When one grows up, he still appreciates approval by others, but still goes on living and working and serving even when there is no recognition by others. Also, gratitude and appreciation of others is one of the flowers of mature love. Love is always glad to say, "Thank you." Also, love feels a deep sense of obligation to others. St. Paul said, "I am debtor both to the Greeks, and to the Barbarians; both to the wise and the unwise" (Romans 1:14). He felt he owed something, not only to those who blessed him, but also to those in need. Love feels its obligation to serve.

Love puts away childish things—it grows up.

THE GRAND CLIMAX

St. Paul closes this, the most complete statement on love in existence, with a grand climax in verse 13: "And now abideth faith, hope, love, these three: but the greatest of these is love."

Underscore that word *abideth*. Make a list of the things people are seeking today, and we see that so many of these are temporary —clothes that will be out of style next year, cars that will wear out, treasures that "moth and rust doth corrupt." So often we are disappointed in the things we possess because we realize they are for such a short duration. Every material possession will one day

be lost, physical strength will one day become weakness, the years
will steal away our beauty. The most brilliant career will come to
an end. The most thunderous applause will die into silence. The
satisfaction we have in our possessions today is no guarantee that
we will be satisfied tomorrow.

How much better to possess some things that *abideth*—things
that will endure no matter what happens. St. Paul names three
things that we can hold onto forever: **Faith, Hope, and Love.**

FAITH

Without faith, life is a difficult journey. Without faith, we are
never quite sure of ourselves. Without faith, it is difficult to make
decisions. Without faith, we are afraid to dare, to dream, to
adventure. Failing to possess faith, we look at our fellow man with
suspicion and cynicism. We miss the comfort and stimulation of
real friendships. We think the world is against us. We lose our
enthusiasm for living.

Without faith, we lose our great ideals and purposes, and life
takes on a lower tone. Without faith, we become possessed with
a what's-the-use attitude.

There are many definitions of faith, but essentially it means two
things: first, to continue to believe no matter what happens. One
of the grandest statements St. Paul made was this one: "I have
kept the faith." Life dealt harshly with him, but through it all,
he held fast to certain firm convictions. He was faithful to his
highest principles, and in being faithful, he never lost his faith.

The other part of faith is that when we face up to life and know
that we are unable to conquer life in our own strength, we can
depend on a higher help. Faith means three things about God:

(1) God created this world. It also means that God
controls this world. For a time it may seem that evil

will triumph, but remember, "This is my Father's world."

(2) Faith means God cares. There come times when one feels forgotten and deserted, left out and alone. I wrote a boy who was located thousands of miles away. He wrote back, "Your letter made me feel that I had not been forgotten." This assurance gives inspiration for living.

(3) Faith means God is working with us, and not just watching us from afar. This does not mean that everything that happens is good, or according to His will. Sometimes God's will can be temporarily defeated. But God continues to work, and God will triumph.

In this connection, we recall a conversation from *The Big Fisherman* by Lloyd C. Douglas.

"Don't forget," admonished Peter, "that we couldn't understand why he wanted to leave Canaan and come to Capernaum."

"That was different," mumbled Thomas. "He felt that he was urgently needed there." "Maybe he feels that he is now needed elsewhere," observed Andrew, to which James added, "I don't believe he cares very much whether we understand him or not."

"You are right, Jimmy," rumbled old Bartholomew. "He's teaching us to have faith in him."

"But—can't a man have faith—and understanding, too?" argued Thomas.

"No!" declared Bartholomew, bluntly. "That's what faith is for, my son! It's for when we can't understand!"

"That's true!" approved Peter. "When a man under-
stands, he doesn't need any faith."

"I don't like to be kept in the dark," put in Philip.

"If a man has enough faith," replied Peter, "he can
find his way in the dark—with faith as his lamp."

Even in the midst of confusion, doubt, and failure of understanding, faith abideth.

HOPE

Hope is something else that will abide. Many people have so
watered down hope that it represents little more than wishful
thinking. But hope is something big and strong and sturdy. It is
a firm expectation based on certain fundamental truths and actions. Hope is never a substitute for clear thinking and hard work.
On the contrary, hope leads one to think and to work.

When one becomes discouraged, when life looks utterly dark,
when all one's plans have failed, then there is a choice of one of
three ways out.

(1) There is the way of the fool. The Bible tells us,
"The fool hath said in his heart, there is no God
..." (Psalms 14:1). This way looks at difficult situations
and sees nothing but hopelessness. Seeing no hope, this
person simply says, "I will quit ... I don't like this job,
I'll get another one ... This thrill has let me down, I
will seek another one ... There are some problems in
my marriage, I will break it up ... I cannot face this
situation, I will run away from it." Having no hope, a
person can have nothing to hold onto.

(2) A second way to face the troubles of life is the
cynic's way. It is a little better than the fool's way but

not much better. The cynic believes everything turns out bad. "This is just my luck," he says. "There is no joy in life for me, I'll just bear it the best I can." The cynic never expects much, and thus he is never very disappointed. He is simply resigned to life.

(3) A third way to face life is the way of hope. Of course, there will be disappointments and setbacks, but hope sees the sunshine following the storm. God gave us ears to hear with because there is music to be heard. The Christian believes that. Also, he believes God gave us eyes because there is beauty to be seen. Also, he believes God gave us the ability to hope because there is something finer and better ahead, and if we keep going, we shall find it.

> Hope, like a gleaming taper's light,
> Adorns and cheers our way:
> And still, as darker grows the night,
> Emits a brighter ray.

OLIVER GOLDSMITH, *The Captivity*

LOVE

Love is the third thing that *abideth*. But it is more than just the third thing: "The greatest of these is love." And, love is what this book is all about.

2

When One Is Love-Starved

A mother asked her husband to care for the children one Saturday afternoon while she went shopping. The father happened to be a statistician. When she returned, the husband handed her a record of the afternoon:

> dried the children's tears—14 times
> tied their shoe laces—16 times
> served drinks of water—22 times
> toy balloons blown—3 per child
> average life of balloon—12 seconds
> cautioned children not to cross the street—34 times
> children insisted on crossing street—34 times
> number of Saturdays father will do this in the future—
> NONE

I sympathize with the poor fellow. For most parents, there is no sweeter hour than when they finally get their children to sleep and can sit down and rest for a little while.

But it is simply a matter of fact that many times we will give our children everything—plenty of food, a good bed, an education, toys of all kinds, plenty of spending money—everything except just one thing, ourselves. Missing that one thing, they miss everything.

If love is given to a child as it has a right to expect, then the child may be punished for its wrongs, denied many other advantages, even an education and a good time generally, yet that child receiving love will grow to be a happy and emotionally well-balanced child.

Gipsy Smith told about one of his boys coming into his study one day while he was very busy. He offered to let the boy borrow his knife, but the boy refused it. He offered him a number of things. Finally he asked, "Son, what do you *want?*" The boy replied, "Daddy, I just want you."

I tell that not as a sentimental story. Rather does it illustrate the most basic desire of a child, and, missing that *you,* the child misses everything. That is an explanation of many of the maladjusted people today.

I was interested recently in reading of a movie which was shown to a New York City meeting of health educators. Its purpose was to show that babies need love as much as they need food, and it traced the mental wasting of ninety-one well-fed babies in a South American orphanage.

The orphanage provided adequate food, clothing, and all the material needs. However, the home had only a few nurses and they did not have time to give to the babies love and attention. The result was that twenty-seven died in their first year, seven in the second, while another twenty-seven developed into adults with deep mental problems.

Dr. J. A. Hadfield, of London University, published a book supporting the theory that mental and emotional disturbances in later life are mainly due to a lack of proper love and understanding in childhood. Of course, there are many causes of emotional upsets, but certainly, lack of love is a major cause.

SOME RESENT EVERYBODY

Let me give an actual example. A lady about thirty-five years old came to me as an alcoholic. I certainly am no expert on alcoholism but I have done the best I could to help some. In every instance where I have seen progress made, it came by finding a cause for the emotional unbalance that resulted in alcoholism.

This lady talked to me about how wrong everything is. She did not like Houston. The people here are snooty, she claimed, and she planned to move. The company she works for is heartless and cruel, she said. Her boss is mean to her and goes out of his way to make her work unpleasant.

She refused to go to church because church people are all self-righteous and are unfriendly. She divorced her husband because he put his own people before her. He was kind and good to his mother and neglected her, she told me.

She finally told me that her own family had always treated her mean. She never wanted to see her mother or father again. I discovered that when she was born, her parents had set their hearts on having a son. When a girl came, they were disappointed.

Ten years later, another baby came into that home, and it was a boy. He was named for his father. He was adored and every attention was given him. The little girl was somewhat pushed aside. The mother would read to them, holding the little boy in her lap while the girl would sit in a chair by herself.

By the time she was eighteen or twenty, she was starved. Doctors tell us that if we do not eat properly, our stomachs will shrink to the point that we become incapable of eating a full meal. So with our affection. One can reach the point where the capacity to either love or be loved is wasted away.

No wonder the girl found an unfriendly and unloving world.

Wherever she goes it will be the same. And humans as we are, life without love is unlivable. In her case, the oblivion provided by alcohol became one means by which life was bearable.

Because she was denied love as a child, she would not accept love from any person in later life. However, a love-starved person might take an exact opposite course.

RESENT NOBODY

Instead of resenting everybody, they resent nobody. Their one desire is the approval of other people. Any criticism from any source worries them almost to distraction. A love-starved person may do most anything to gain popularity and fame. Public approval and publicity become intoxicants just as complete as alcohol.

MISANTHROPY

The love-starved person may turn to misanthropy, which is a dislike or distrust of mankind. The same person may spend his life in a false philanthropy, claiming to love mankind and rendering all manner of services for the betterment of people, when all the time, he is not concerned with helping others; he is merely seeking a substitute for the love he missed.

Study, for example, the writings and life of Hitler. He screamed with evangelical fervor his desires to put bread into the mouths of hungry people, when all of the time, he was really seeking to build up his own love-starved ego. All his talk about a master race was merely a screen behind which he was seeking the glory of men for himself.

But no amount of fame or public applause ever takes the place of warm, genuine human love.

SYMPATHY

Lacking love, some people seek sympathy. They are never well and they are always happy to tell of all their aches and pains to any who will listen. Life is never so sweet than it is when they are being martyred. If there is no one to mistreat and hurt them, then often this person will line up fiercely in some unpopular cause.

There is legitimate crusading, but sometimes crusading is merely a method one uses to get himself martyred. He feels that the spilling of his own blood will arouse sympathetic concern on the part of his fellows. There are those who will never rest, because you cannot get sympathy from others while you are resting. It is when you are overworking that someone may take pity on you. And that pity becomes a crumb of bread for the hunger of one's heart for love.

There was a girl who was jilted by her sweetheart. The thought of being unwanted and unloved made her desperate. Subconsciously she told herself, "If I were ill, I would get sympathy." She began to have fainting spells at the office. They were not faked —they were real.

If one does not have enough to eat, his body becomes weak and he is susceptible to fainting. And when one's spirit becomes weakened (in this case because of not having sufficient love), it also may faint. It is no less real than fainting from physical weakness.

When the girl was made to understand her condition and given the proper course of treatment, she immediately became well.

LEARNING TO LOVE

"I am killing myself because I have never sincerely loved any human being in my life," wrote a young woman in explanation of her suicide. Many people are killing themselves because they have never learned to love.

There was a woman who twice had been committed to an institution for the mentally ill. Fearing another breakdown, she decided to go back to the small town of her girlhood for a visit. She had not been back since she first went away to college.

She spent the summer there with an old lady who had known her family since before she was born. The old grandmother told the younger woman much family history—how she was an unwanted child, treated coldly. "I used to feel so sorry for you when you were a little tyke," said the grandmother. "A child needs love if it is to grow right. Just as an adult must have love if he is to keep sane."

This opened a new world of fact for the woman and sent her searching for other facts. She began to learn some of the nature of God—that God who is love. She learned there can be no growth without love. She learned that when one selects a life of lonely selfishness that one is also cutting off the warm mental stimulation which gives zest to living.

The wise old grandmother convinced the younger woman that she would never lose her mind if she could only get enough people to love her, to care about what happened to her. Then the grandmother told her to substitute thoughts of helping others for her fears of another mental breakdown. As she learned to love, she became a sane, balanced, and well person.

That is the pathway for one to follow who has been love-starved. I have talked with many people privately who are literally starving for love. They are bitter and resentful. Some have the spirit of Frederick the Great. One day he struck a subject with a whip and exclaimed: "Confound you: I want you to love me." But love is not something which can be commanded.

A definition of love which won a nationwide newspaper contest reads: LOVE IS THE DOORWAY THROUGH WHICH THE HUMAN SOUL PASSES FROM SELFISHNESS TO SERVICE AND FROM SOLITUDE TO KINSHIP WITH ALL MANKIND.

There is only one way to make up for the love you have missed:
That one way is by loving. The words of Christ can be para-
phrased to read: "He that saveth his love shall lose it but he that
loseth his love for others shall find it."

Try it. Try it today. Here is how: Think of one who irritates
you, someone you do not love. Pray for that one right now, calling
the name in your prayer. During the day, study that person. What
are some of his or her good qualities? What are some of his or her
bad qualities? Try to figure out *why* that person has that bad
quality. Be an amateur psychiatrist and analyze the cause of those
things in that person that cause you not to love him or her.
Resolve to love that one "in spite of" even if you cannot love him
"on account of."

Try to gain that one victory of love. You will feel a lot better.
Try it and see.

3

Love Overcomes Destructive Emotions

"Perfect love casteth out fear," said St. John in the long ago (1 John 4:18). And modern medicine and psychology have finally caught up with the Bible and confirmed that truth. John is talking about the two strongest emotions of the human system—love and fear—and he says love has the power to destroy fear.

Physicians today tell us that from 50 to 75 percent of all of our sickness is caused by our emotions. Emotion is simply the ability to feel. Keep telling yourself that you feel sick and you will be sick. If you are sick, more than half of the time your sickness will be cured simply by convincing yourself that you feel well.

We have physical bodies and we also have feelings or emotions. Basically all of our emotions are good, but if any of them get out of control, then they are bad. Like fire. Fire is one of the greatest benefactors of man. But uncontrolled fire can burn up a man's house, and even the man himself.

There are four main groups of destructive emotions. Actually, even these emotions are good as long as we can control them, but when we let them get out of hand, they make us sick in many ways.

(1) There is the *fear* group, including anxiety, worry, and apprehension.

(2) *Anger* is the father of another group of destructive emotions. Some of the children of anger are hostility, resentment, envy, jealousy, and hatred. However, anger is closely related to fear because we do not feel hostile toward a person until we become afraid that person can hurt us in some way.

(3) A third group of destructive emotions is headed up by what we feel as a *sense of failure*. This leads to such things as discouragement, depressed moods, and various guilt feelings. Without this family of emotions, there would be no repentance, but they also lead to self-destruction.

(4) *Pride* is the captain of another army of sickening emotions, including prejudice, selfishness, self-consciousness, and conceit.

When St. John says, "Perfect love casteth out fear," I think that by fear he has in mind *all* of the destructive emotions, because they are all a part of fear or stem from fear. And when he talks about love, he means all of the healing emotions, because love is the basis of them all.

There is faith, which makes us believe. And hope, which keeps us looking upward and forward. ". . . but the greatest of these is love," said St. Paul (1 Corinthians 13:13). And God's Book tells us that if you have perfect love in your heart, it will drive out your fears and worries, your angers and jealousies, your failures and guilts, and make you a well-balanced, and happy person.

In other words, St. John says the only way to destroy our sickening emotions is developing our healing emotions.

Jesus tells the story (Matthew 24:14–30) of a man who had three servants. Before the man left on a long journey, he gave to one of his servants five talents, to another two, and to another one. Two of the servants invested their talents in such a way to double them.

But the third servant did not use his. When the man returned, he highly complimented the two servants who did so well. But he had harsh words indeed for the servant who did nothing. In explaining his failure, the servant said, "I was afraid" (v. 25).

One of our most sickening fears is that fear of failure. That fear has made invalids out of many healthy people.

We have made success one of our gods and we fall down and worship before it. Parents are often overly ambitious for their children. Not having reached the goals in life they desired, they relive those ambitions in their children, seeking a vicarious satisfaction as the child succeeds.

And many children have been driven into this paralyzing fear of failure. I have talked with people who were afraid to attempt even the simplest undertakings. Often you find that parents or teachers ridiculed them as children for even the smallest of failures. Many children have had this fear instilled in them by being unfavorably compared with more brilliant or capable children.

That is always the wrong approach. A person hungers for appreciation just as he hungers for bread, and without appreciation, no person can be his best. Some people think that if you compliment a person it will make him conceited. That is not true.

Look into your own heart and you will see that expressed appreciation makes you humble, never conceited. But because our hunger for appreciation is so great, if we do not receive it from others, we will bestow it upon ourselves. We will praise and magnify ourselves and self-conceit is the result. Conversely, when this basic hunger for appreciation is received from others, one becomes truly humble.

A friend of mine tells of a boy who was a problem child from the time he was in the first grade. Almost every teacher he had assumed he was a hopeless case. It was discovered the boy's parents had a cruel tendency to find fault. The boy was beaten, shouted at, and ridiculed for his mistakes. At sixteen the boy had quit school and he went to work for the manager of an amusement park.

The manager was not a trained psychologist, but he did have a kind, understanding heart. He was a man of love, and it was natural for him to praise and thank the boy for each job which he did well. Little by little the boy quit thinking of failure as he began receiving the one thing for which his heart had been longing.

A little appreciating love cast out his fear.

I have the case histories of two women who had almost identical operations. One of the women was a shy, sensitive, over-protected person. The operation was very successful, but the lady was constantly depressed. She talked constantly of "the terrible thing" which had happened to her. She talked about how she would never be able to take care of herself. Three or four weeks after the operation she died.

As far as the operation was concerned, the case of the other woman was the same. However, her operation had been postponed until her baby was born. Her operation was performed two weeks later. In two more weeks, she was at home and soon she was completely recovered.

She had no time to lie around a hospital and pamper herself. She had a baby and that baby needed her. The deepest feeling she had was her love for that baby. I cannot write a definition of perfect love, but the love of a mother for her baby is the best example of perfect love that I know. Her love cast out all her fears about herself, and instead of dying as did the first woman, she quickly was healed.

There was a girl who was brought to a hospital and died within a short time. Following the autopsy, the physician said to the girl's mother, "We could find no cause of death." The mother replied, "Oh, doctor, you don't have to tell me why she died. She died of a broken heart. The young man to whom she was engaged was killed a few weeks ago. Since that time she has had no interest in anything."

Of a broken heart. That means she had lost her love. Very often, the loss of love means the loss of security, maybe the loss of self-respect. Frequently when love is crushed, one becomes overwhelmed with the feeling of being not needed or not wanted. And that can be and often is fatal. It can destroy in a person any desire to live, and consciously or subconsciously that person begins to desire death. The desire for death becomes stronger than the instinct for self-preservation. Thus one *does* die of a broken heart.

The cure: Jesus said, ". . . he that loseth his life for my sake shall find it" (Matthew 10:39). Or again, ". . . seek ye first the kingdom of God, and his righteousness; and all these things shall be added unto you" (Matthew 6:33).

That is, when you give yourself to something greater than yourself, when some great cause becomes more important than your own life, and to that cause you give all of your interests and feelings, then that cause will give back to you a stronger and healthier life than you ever experienced before.

Self-centeredness makes us sick. Perfect love heals us.

Abraham Lincoln and his law partner, William Herndon, were arguing the question of whether or not any person ever performs a completely unselfish act. They were riding together through the country and came upon a pig caught in a rail fence. Herndon pretended not to see the animal and passed on by.

But Lincoln stopped, got down and waded through a muddy ditch, pulled the rails apart and released the pig. Herndon pointed triumphantly to Lincoln's muddy shoes and spattered trousers, saying, "You see now I am right. Men are capable of performing unselfish deeds."

"Oh no," replied Lincoln, "if I had left that pig in the fence, I would have worried about him all night. I would have been so busy wondering if someone had rescued him, or if he was still held between those rails, that I would have lost my sleep. For my own peace of mind, I had to rescue the animal. So, you see, I was merely being selfish."

Without entering the argument of Lincoln and Herndon as to whether or not a person is capable of performing a completely unselfish act, that story does illustrate the fact that, failure to give may sometimes be very costly. In Lincoln's case, it would have cost him a night's sleep and his peace of mind.

"For God so loved the world that He gave. . . ." Love is a process of giving. In fact, love demands expression, and if it is not expressed, it becomes a poison for one's own soul.

But in order to have love come into our lives, first we must express our love for others. "The song is to the singer, and comes back most to him; The gift is to the giver, and comes back most to him; The love is to the lover, and comes back most to him."

". . . With what measure ye mete, it shall be measured unto you . . ." said Jesus (Mark 4:24). Again, He said, "Give, and it shall be given unto you . . ." (Luke 6:38).

". . . perfect love casteth out fear . . ." says St. John (1 John 4:18). What is the basis of fear? I think it is the possibility of losing—losing health, security, friends, or any of many things. If you have nothing to lose, then you have nothing to fear.

Perfect love gives without thought of return. Therefore, love has nothing to lose. Love has already given all that it has. Thus, love has nothing to fear. Love does cast out fear.

4

You Can Stake Your Life on Love

"For God so loved . . ."—that is the greatest statement in the Bible (John 3:16). It is the revelation of the character of God, the explanation of the laws that control the world in which we live, and the foundation upon which every successful life must be built.

No wonder the Bible warns us that even though one might have marvelous gifts and graces, talents and wealth, if that person does not have love, he is nothing. And, even though one might do many wonderful things and even give his life in service, there is no profit in such a life, unless that person possesses love (1 Corinthians 13:1–3). Love, and love alone, determines any person's worth and any person's success in this business of living. Love is the most important thing in life.

You may not understand much of the Bible. You may not be able to quote the Apostle's Creed or even the Lord's Prayer. You may have become the victim of sin. Your mind might be filled with doubt and despair. Even in spite of those things, you are still within the reach of God. But if you ever reach the point of killing all the love in your heart, then you become a pitiful creature, most miserable and without hope.

On the other hand, you may have an educated mind, give your talents in many worthwhile services, rise to places of prominence in the eyes of other people, live an honorable and decent life, but even after you have done all these things, if you have left love out of your life, you are a useless person and life for you is a failure. The absence of love is the explanation of the unhappiness and restlessness of vast multitudes of people today. Love is the one quality of character—the only one—about which we can say, "If a person has this, his life is good—without this, no matter what else he may have or do, life is bad."

EROS

What is love? That word has been used to describe so many things that we have become confused as to its real meaning. The Greeks had a word *eros* which we have translated as love. Within the meaning of that word is the act of possessing. It really isn't love, rather is it a perversion of love.

For example, a young man falls in love with a girl. He then wants her entirely for himself. He thinks in terms of making her his. At first, he wants to go steady. That means she must not go with another boy. He wants to hold her close to himself. He wants to make her his wife. For him, that is not love, it is possessing.

Read again Shakespeare's *Othello*. He loved his wife, Desdemona, simply because of what she meant to him. And when he decided she was unfaithful to him, he killed her. So often, when some person does not respond to our love, that love is changed into hatred and, instead of love, we seek or wish for that person some hurt or destruction.

We erroneously think of love in terms of the Greek word *eros* which means possessing for our own good. We remember Jane Carlyle, wife of the great English writer. Some thought she did not love her husband; rather she wanted to be his wife because of his fame and what that would mean to her.

We remember how Scrooge in Dickens' *Christmas Carol* lost

his sweetheart because of his love for gold. Today, we see men neglect their families and everything good and fine in life because of their love for success or position or power. At the very center of such love is self.

Right at this point, we see the fatal error of many people's interest in religion. We pretend we love God, but often it is with an ulterior motive. It isn't God we want—instead we want peace of mind, or power in life, or the answer to our prayers, or we want to escape hell, or we want God's providences. And, so often, when something upsetting happens to us, we turn away from our faith in bitter resentment.

Here is a parent whose child died. As a result, that parent becomes filled with self-pity, or resentment, or doubt, and becomes an altogether unlovely person. That parent did not truly love. Instead, it merely possessed.

AGAPE

But there is another word which we also translate as love. It is the word of the New Testament, *agape*. That love is never focused on one's self, but rather upon the object of love. Its meaning is not found in possessing, but in just the opposite—in giving. "For God so loved the world that he gave . . ." (John 3:16).

Why did God make this world? Why did He make me? I often have wondered why He made us. I have been a bother to Him, and time and again I have disappointed Him. The real answer to why He made any of us is not because of what we can do for Him but because of what He can do for us. We came not because of necessity, but because of love. A couple may have a baby because they are lonely and because life for them has grown stale and empty. They feel a baby will put back into their lives what they have lost. On the other hand, a couple may have a baby because they have so much to give and they are not satisfied until they do give. You can have a baby for what it can do for you, or for what you can do for the baby. God made us for what He can do for us. That is the true expression of love.

LAWS OF LOVE

Now—that leads me to the very heart of this matter of love. Because the world, and all that is within it, is an expression of the love of God, then we can be sure that the world is governed by the laws of love. And if we are to really find life in its truest and fullest meaning, we must follow the pathways of love.

Suppose you took a trip to Alaska in the middle of the winter. Would you carry the same clothes that you would carry to Florida in the summer—thin cotton shirts or dresses, open shoes, your bathing suit, and no overcoat? No—one must adjust himself to the climate in which he lives, otherwise he would not survive.

So one must adjust himself to the spiritual environment of his world. The same God who made our physical world also made our spiritual world. We know that if we eat arsenic, we will die. Yet, we foolishly forget that when we put into our lives hatred, jealousy, selfishness, resentments, unforgiving spirits and the like, we kill the spirit of God within us. This is what the Bible means when it says, ". . . the soul that sinneth, it shall die" (Ezekiel 18:4).

MAN'S REDEMPTION

Now I come to man's chief problem. Many have despaired of our race. Many people believe man is a hopeless creature, that he cannot be redeemed. We have come to believe that self-assertion is one of our basic instincts. Put your finger into the hand of a tiny baby and it will hold tightly to it. And as one grows, that possessive instinct grows with him and becomes the chains of his life. His ambitions lie in taking care of himself, possessing the things he wants, obtaining security for himself, doing the things that bring him pleasure. Those ambitions, we know, eventually result in frustration, but we seem powerless to do anything about them. True love is the surrendering of our very selves, and that is something man is unable to do by the exercise of his own will power.

And therein lies the redemption of the Cross of Christ. Read again the life story of Teresa. For forty years she had been a very practical person living for herself, taking care of herself, getting what she could for herself. Though she was living in a convent, still she was living for herself. But one day, she became different. It happened in a moment.

As she walked along a hallway, she saw a picture of the Lord being scourged. She must have seen that picture a hundred times, but this time she saw it as she had never seen it before. She saw God suffering—suffering for love and for her. She fell on her knees. She arose a new soul. She said she arose with "a sense of unpayable debt," and all the balance of her life was different.

In many forms, and sometimes even in the most unlikely moments, that experience may come. We have gone along our self-seeking ways. We have known about Christ but we have never really seen Him. And then it happens, and we know what it means to be redeemed by His blood. Then we realize that His way is *the* Way. Instead of ourselves, He becomes the center of life for us. To Him we give ourselves, and we begin to walk the pathway of true love. Then we find life.

STAKED HIS LIFE ON LOVE

When one really loves God, then no sacrifice for God becomes too great.

Look at Henry Martyn, who has been called the "most heroic figure in the English Church since the time of Queen Elizabeth I." After a brilliant career at Cambridge, he heard the call to the mission field and tossed aside half a dozen possible careers to answer that call. He prepared himself for India in a spirit of complete dedication.

Then something else happened. He fell deeply in love with a girl named Lydia. He told her of his love for her and also of his orders from heaven. Would she go with him? Together, they could do great things for God.

She would not go. If he stayed in England she would marry him. If he went to India, he must go alone. So the question hammered in his brain: "India or Lydia? Lydia or India?"

He chose aright. He went to India and he went alone. He never again knew such love as he had known for Lydia. She married someone else and forever was beyond his love. For the remainder of his life there was the burden of that disappointment. Yet in the midst of that pain he said, "My dear Lydia and my duty called me different ways. Yet God hath not forsaken me. I am born for God only. Christ is nearer to me than father or mother, or sister." And I am sure he could have added, "Than Lydia, either."

There was a man who staked his life on love—love that thinks not of itself or what it can gain, but love which thinks only of what it can give. Would you say that in the end he won or that he lost?

I say it reverently and prayerfully, but God also staked His life on love. "For God so loved the world, that he gave his only begotten Son . . ." (John 3:16). I know He suffered and died because He followed the course of love, but would you say that in the end God won or that He lost?

The choice of Henry Martyn or the choice of Christ's Cross does not often come to many Christians—yet, usually we face the choice to some degree. To follow the pathway of God's love may mean the giving up of this possession, or that pleasure, or the rendering of this service, or walking in this way of life.

Sometimes the choice boils down to simply: If I follow the pathway of love, I must take the chance of not living for myself, but living for Him. Can I afford to take that chance? Or must I first put my own needs and interest? And I answer that with the assurance, you *can* afford to stake your life on love.

5

The Three Life-Determining Principles

What is going to happen in the future? A lot of people are wondering and a lot of people are afraid. I find many who are haunted by discouragement and despair. They see nothing good ahead. Many people see no reason in living, but one does not have to be the victim of tomorrow. I am one who believes one can take a firm hold of his future and be the master of it.

The Bible says, "And now abideth faith, hope and love . . ." (1 Corinthians 13:13). In that sentence, we have laid down the three basic principles of determining your own life—faith, hope, love. Let those words sink into your mind and become a part of you. They will lead you into a life that is successful in the very highest and best sense.

First—Learn to have *faith*. The first cause of failure is lack of faith. Failure and faith are incompatible words—they just cannot exist together. If you have faith, you will not fail; if you fail, it is a sign you do not have faith. Faith may have setbacks but faith never knows failure. Faith loses battles but does not lose the war.

The famous football coach, Knute Rockne, had four rules for the selection of the boys on his great Notre Dame teams: He said, "(1) I will not have a boy with a swelled head for you cannot teach him anything. (2) I will not have a griper, kicker, or complainer. (3) I will allow no dissipation. (4) I will not have a boy with an inferiority complex; he must believe he can accomplish things."

Read again number four of Rockne's rules. It is the most important. The psychologist William James, who probably better understood people than any American who ever lived, confirmed Mr. Rockne's rule. He said, "Our belief at the beginning of a doubtful undertaking is the one thing [note that he said the *one* thing] that assures the successful outcome of our venture."

But faith is not something that suddenly comes to a person in some magical manner. It is something that must be learned. The best guide I know for learning faith is contained in these words from the Bible: "Jesus said unto him, If thou canst believe, all things are possible to him that believeth. And straightway the father of the child cried out and said with tears, Lord, I believe..." (Mark 9:23,24).

The first step is to get the word *impossible* out of our vocabulary. We begin losing faith by saying, "It can't be done," or something similar. We begin learning faith by believing it *can* be done. Here is a little plan that works wonders. Keep count of the times in one day you say or think something is impossible. At the end of the day write that number down.

The next day, concentrate on reducing the times you allowed yourself to think in that negative fashion. See how many times you reduced the number of the previous day. Continue day by day to reduce your use of *impossible*. Gradually more and more areas of your life move into the realm of the possible. You develop new courage and strength as faith begins to grow within you. Try it and you will see.

But that is not the full answer. Notice, the man replied, "Lord, I believe." To merely say, "I believe," tremendously increases one's power, but to begin with *Lord* is far greater. In fact, true faith must begin with God. We recall that Jesus said, "The things which are impossible with men are possible with God" (Luke 18:27).

The longer I live, the less confidence I have in myself, but the more confidence I have in God. I am conscious of my own weaknesses and limitations but I have become increasingly conscious of God's strength and power. And as I shift my confidence from myself to God, I find my faith becoming stronger. Somehow —I don't always see how, but I know that *somehow*—God will always know what to do and has the power to do it. That gives me faith.

"Faith, hope, and love"—I wrote of the power of faith so let us next consider *hope*. One of the finest pieces of literature is Tennyson's *In Memoriam*. In it we find these words: "The mighty hopes that make us men." Truly, hope is one of the ingredients it takes to make a man.

You are familiar with G. F. Watts's picture entitled *Hope*. It pictures a poor woman against the world. Her eyes are bandaged so that she cannot see ahead. In her hands is a harp, but all the strings are broken save one. Those broken strings represent her shattered expectations, her bitter disappointments. That one last unbroken string is the string of hope. She strikes that string and a glorious melody floats out over her world; it fills her dark skies with stars. The artist painted a great truth: Even when all else is gone, you still can have hope, and no one is defeated until hope is gone.

Dr. Samuel Johnson, the brilliant English man of letters, said that to have a bright, hopeful outlook on life is worth a thousand pounds a year. That is, when one thinks with hope, he will attain far more. Certainly there is much evidence to cause one to believe that the attitude of one's mind determines what happens to him. Job said, ". . . that which I was afraid of is come unto me" (3:25). Many are able to say, "That which I hoped has come to pass."

I have a friend who has a deep aversion to hearing anyone use profanity. In his pocket he carries a supply of little cards which he hands out to those he thinks needs them. On the card is printed these words:

The use of PROFANITY is the sublime effort of the ignorant, uncouth, simple-minded, godless man to express himself—"Thou shalt not take the name of the Lord thy God in vain; for the Lord will not hold him guiltless that taketh his name in vain" (Exodus 20:7).

I am in hearty sympathy with my friend's campaign against profanity. It is the most useless—and one of man's worst—habits. But, as I frequently point out, the worst profanity is not the swear words people use. The most profane word is *hopeless*. The Bible says, "Hope thou in God . . ." (Psalm 42:5). To become hopeless is to deny God.

Hope is not a dreamy, unreal thing. It is based on the most real thing there is—the existence of the Almighty, Eternal God. The Psalmist said, "Why art thou cast down, O my soul? And why art thou disquieted in me? Hope thou in God: for I shall yet praise Him for the help of His countenance" (Psalm 42:5). That is to say, when you are disheartened, put God in the center of your thoughts. By concentrating on your troubles, you despair; by concentrating on God, you hope. If you will do that, the day will come when you will have reason to praise God.

It has been well said: "Life is full of glad surprises for those who hope."

"Faith, hope, and love. . . ." Take that word *love*. Wrapped up in it is so much: unselfishness, good will, kindness. No person can live unto himself. The reaction of other people in so many ways determines what our own lives will turn out to be. And love toward others is always the best way to follow.

One of my favorite stories is tucked away in the Book of Genesis. Joseph had been sold into slavery by his jealous brothers. Later Joseph had become the king's chief assistant down in Egypt. Due to the famine in their land, these brothers had gone to Egypt to beg for food. They did not recognize their brother Joseph, but he told them to bring with them their brother Benjamin the next time they came.

This grieved their father Jacob. Since he had lost Joseph, young Benjamin had become dear to his heart. Fearful they might keep Benjamin in Egypt, Jacob had his sons carry gifts for the Egyptians—balm, spices and myrrh, nuts, fruit, and a double amount of money. And the old man also said, ". . . take a little honey" (Genesis 43:11). Honey represents something sweet and gentle.

To make the most of life, we need to take along ability, training, initiative, faith and hope—also, don't forget to ". . . take a little honey." A kinder, sweeter spirit always wins in the long run.

You remember the old story about how the sun and the wind got into an argument about which was the stronger. The wind said to the sun, "I am stronger. All you do is shine, but I blow, and believe me, when I blow everybody knows it."

They saw a man walking down the road. They agreed they would test their strengths by seeing which could make the man take off his coat. The wind went to work, but the harder it blew, the closer the man pulled his coat around him. Then came the sun's turn to try. It made no noise; it just quietly began to send warm rays toward the man, and pretty soon the man had his coat off.

That is a silly little story but it illustrates a great truth. Simple, warm, loving kindness works wonders. The Bible tells us, "Be ye kind one to another, tenderhearted, forgiving one another, even as God for Christ's sake hath forgiven you" (Ephesians 4:32). Isn't it true that kindness will accomplish so much more than the pugnacious, hard-boiled attitude? Then wouldn't it be a good idea for us to start practicing it a little more?

Robert Louis Stevenson said a wonderful thing: "Anyone can carry his burden, however heavy, until nightfall. Anyone can do his work, however hard, for one day. Anyone can live sweetly, patiently, lovingly, purely till the sun goes down. And this is all life really means."

6

Love—the Foundation of the Family

Jesus told a story about two men who built houses. One built his house on a rock—a firm foundation. The other built on the sand—a very *unfirm* foundation. Both houses got along fine for a time, but then the rains descended, the floods came, and the winds blew. The house on the rock stood: the house on the sand fell (Matthew 7:24–27).

To begin with, that simple story illustrates the need of building a house on a firm foundation. But we need to go beyond that. Also, we need a firm foundation for the home which we plan to put into our houses. A house can be washed away in a flood, blown away by a tornado, burned up by a fire. It is bad for a house to be destroyed.

But even worse is for a *home* to be destroyed—and homes can be destroyed by so many enemies:

Disagreements over money is one thing that can destroy a home.

Conflicts with one's in-laws can also destroy a home. Ever so often, I have heard someone say, "I married him; I did not marry his family." But that is not true. When one marries another person, he or she marries that other person's family also, and any other idea can bring trouble.

Different interests or a lack of common interest is something else that can destroy a home.

Failure of adjustments in the intimate marriage relation can also be fatally damaging.

Disagreements over children can shake a home's foundations.

Husbands and wives can lose their tempers.

Harsh words can be spoken, and the home foundations go crumbling down.

Alcohol and dope can be the basis of a home-destroying storm.

Religion is one of the foundations of a home, but religious differences can make that foundation crack.

Sooner or later, just like every house must face up to some storm, every home will also have its storms to face.

The sad truth is more than half the homes fail to survive. When a home falls, not only are the marriage partners hurt, often children and others are scarred for life.

There are many foundations of a home, but here let us concern ourselves with the one foundation which is the most important —and that is love. In fact, if a home has this foundation and no other, it still has a good chance for survival. But, it can have all other foundations and lack this foundation of love and fall into destruction.

Once a man consulted a psychiatrist about the best thing he could do for his children. He had made a list, including such things as: providing material necessities, such as food, clothes, house, and all the others; assuring an opportunity for education; making available religious training; instilling in the children proper social attitudes; setting a good moral example.

The psychiatrist said, "All these are extremely important, but you have not named the most important thing you can do for your children."

The man wondered aloud what was more important than the things he had named.

"The best thing you can do for your children," replied the psychiatrist, "is love their mother."

I think that is a wise statement, because children are alive to the kind of affection there is between father and mother. Nothing gives them a deeper sense of security than to know their parents love each other. Nothing shakes them quite as much as to realize love is lacking between the two adults they depend on the most.

One of the ministers I have loved and appreciated the most across the years has been Dr. Pierce Harris, who is now in the Father's House. When I first started in the ministry, I heard him preach. He captured me that day, and I've looked up to him ever since. For more than twenty-five years, he was pastor of the First Methodist Church in Atlanta, Georgia. Great multitudes of people were inspired by his ministry.

I shall never forget one night while I was living in Atlanta, Georgia. It was about one o'clock in the morning. A man from a radio station phoned to tell me that Dr. and Mrs. Harris had been in an automobile wreck, and that she was killed. I asked him where it happened, and he told me near Eatonton, Georgia. It was about seventy miles away. I hurriedly dressed and drove down there and located the hospital. I went quietly into his room, thinking he might be asleep. He was laying there in pain, but wide awake. As I came in the door, he said, "Charles, you ought not to have come down here tonight—but I knew you would come." I sat with him until daylight, and I shall always cherish those hours in my memory.

We used to travel a lot together to various preaching missions. One of my greatest joys was playing golf with him. He was a very outstanding golfer, and, as we would drive through the country, or walk around some golf course, we used to talk a lot about sermons. He had keen insight and deep wisdom, and from him I gained so much.

Once I had noticed that his subject for the next Sunday was:

"Impressions That Make Life Impossible." That subject intrigued me, and that afternoon on the golf course, as we walked down the first fairway, I asked him about his sermon. He said, "I have four points in that sermon, and when we get to the end of the ninth hole, as we drink a Coca-Cola, I will tell you what they are." I agreed to that, and with some difficulty waited until we had finished nine holes. As we sat resting a few moments, I asked him to give me the "four impressions that make life impossible." As he began telling them to me, I wrote them on the back of our score card. I shall always prize that card. Here they are:

(1) The poisonous impression that only the present is important. He talked a little bit about people who never plan for tomorrow.

(2) The fatal impression that failure is final. He pointed out that one of the chief purposes of preaching was to put hope back into the hearts of those who have lost it. I remember he said, "We need to encourage people to believe that one broken dream is not the end of dreaming."

(3) The dumb impression that drinking isn't dangerous. It was said of Jesus, "The sinners heard him gladly." Dr. Harris was that kind of a man. Many people whose lives had been shattered by liquor and other things came to hear him.

After he had talked about these three impressions that make life impossible, he said, "The fourth is the worst of all." Naturally, I was interested to hear what it was. He got up and said, "Come on; let's finish our golf game, and I will give you that last one when we get into the club house." I really did not enjoy the game as much after that because I was so interested in what the last one might be. After we got into the locker room, we sat down on a bench, and I said, "Now give me that last impression that makes life impossible." He told me:

(4) "The brutal impression that hearts cannot be broken." He said that love is a restless thing, and it seeks constant expression. He told me, "Love is the most delicate flower that grows in the garden of the heart, and it must be carefully cultivated."

Something else he said that day that I put down: "Love never dies; it has to be killed but it can be killed."

I'll never forget that conversation with Dr. Pierce Harris, along with many, many others that we had.

I heard about a man who had what many would say was a rather peculiar habit. For years, he had a special date with his wife every Thursday night. He would come home in the afternoon, shave and shower, put on his best suit, and go out and get in his car and leave. In a little while, he would come back and ring the front doorbell. His wife would greet him at the door, and they would sit for awhile in the living room and talk. Then they would go out to dinner and a show together. They would drive up to the front; he would escort her to the door, kiss her goodnight, and then go drive his car into the garage and come in through the back door.

It sounds sort of silly for a man to do that with his wife—but when that man died, his wife watered his grave with tears.

Falling in love is easy—but *staying* in love has to be worked at.

The other day I turned on the radio in my car and I heard a man singing as he was picking a banjo. The title of one of his songs was, "When the Honeymoon Is Over, the Humdrum of Life Begins." That is the trouble, and that is why a lot of homes crumble and fall. If we expect to keep love alive, we must keep going through the motions of love.

For twenty years now, I have preached each Sunday on television. Many write in and say, "I am a shut-in." They may be old, crippled, or sick. Many of these cannot get out much, and have to stay in the house most of the time.

I have visited and spoken in quite a large number of jails and penitentiaries. It makes me sad to see men and women shut in behind prison bars.

Above most anything else, we Americans want freedom. We do not want to be shut-ins. Young people crave the chance to live their own lives. Women fight for their rights. Husbands or wives do not want to be dominated by the other. We do not want our nation to be governed by a dictator. We want to be free.

But I want to tell you something worse than being a shut-in— that is being a "shut-out."

Some young person may feel restricted by the rules of the parents in the home—but it would be far worse to be an orphan and to have no parents, or to be driven out of the home and not allowed to return.

A husband may feel that his wife is unreasonable and unpleasant and hard to live with—but go back and read Tennyson's story of Enoch Arden. He was considered dead, and his wife married again. He returned home and looked through the window to see his wife with her new husband. The balance of his days, he was a shut-out.

A man may complain about his government and high taxes, but then we remember the man without a country, who was not allowed to be a citizen anywhere.

Love is the opposite of being shut out. Love means acceptance —love means belonging. Love becomes the most important thing in life.

Today we hear a lot about the needs of children and young

people. They need a lot of things, such as being listened to and hearing their side, learning what they are thinking about. They need discipline, but discipline is not enough. One of my best friends wrote these words: "I can remember when mother used to get after us boys. She would take me in the bedroom and talk to me. She would leave me sitting on the edge of the bed, but as she would go out of the room, she would turn around and say, 'But, Son, remember I love you.' That meant more to me than any other thing in my life."

A lot of times children feel shut out. Their parents have not made them feel they were loved. The greatest tragedy is for a child or a youth to feel unwanted and unneeded and unloved.

I talked to a mother just recently whose teen-age daughter is in trouble. She is not married; she is going to have a baby. The mother said a lot of harsh and bitter things to her. She talked about their family's being disgraced. I finally said to the mother, "You stop saying all those bitter things. That girl is hurt enough. You go home and tell that girl, and keep telling her many times every day, that you love her, that you are standing by her, that you are going to help her all the way through." I told that mother, "If you do not love your daughter now, she will likely never need your love again."

When Jesus wanted people to understand what God is like, he told them about a father who welcomed his prodigal son back home. Instead of fussing at the boy, the father ". . . fell on his neck and kissed him" (Luke 15:20).

There are some other foundations a home needs, but if we have love—real love—the other foundations will take care of themselves. Without love, no other foundations are strong enough.

7

Love Thoughts From My Notebook

Man's state is like that of the earth. We think the sun sets and turns itself away from us. But the real fact is that the earth moves away from the sun. The earth would collapse into space if it were not being continually drawn by the sun toward itself. Just so the Sun of Righteousness draws all men to himself by the attraction of his love.

SADHU SUNDAR SINGH

"I hold it true, whate'er befall,
   I feel it, when I sorrow most;
   'Tis better to have loved and lost
Than never to have loved at all."

TENNYSON, *In Memoriam*

Love does not consist in gazing at each other, but in looking outward together in the same direction.

ANTOINE DE SAINT-EXUPÉRY

Some years ago, the *New Yorker* presented a cartoon which shows two young theological students walking within the cloistered walls of the seminary. One of the students has a baffled expression on his countenance, and is remarking to the other: "What gets me about this place is that they want you to love people you don't even like!"

"Do you like dollies?" a little girl asked her house guest. "Yes, very much," the man responded. "Then I'll show you mine," was the reply. Thereupon she presented one by one a whole family of dolls. "And now tell me," the visitor asked, "which is your favorite doll?" The child hesitated for a moment and then said, "You're quite sure you like dollies, and will you please promise not to smile if I show you my favorite?" The man solemnly promised, and the girl hurried from the room. In a moment she returned with a tattered and dilapidated old doll. Its hair had come off; its nose was broken; its cheeks were scratched. An arm and a leg were missing. "Well, well," said the visitor, "and why do you like this one best?" "I love her most," said the little girl, "because if I didn't love her, no one else would."

R. E. THOMAS

A dramatist named Alfred Sutro once wrote a fine, if forgotten, play called *A Maker of Men*, in which a bank clerk returns home, after missing promotion, and says, "I see other men getting on; what have I done?"

His wife answers: "You have made a woman love you. You have given me respect for you, and admiration, and loyalty, and devotion—everything a man can give his wife, except luxury, and that I don't need. Still you call yourself a failure, who within these four walls are the greatest success?"

And Jacob served seven years for Rachel; and they seemed unto him but a few days, for the love he had to her (Genesis 29:20).

"In my country it is understood that a man may love God [said the priest]. It is not a dirty joke."

"I understand" [replied Frederic Henry]. . . .

"You understand but you do not love God."

"No."

"You do not love Him at all?" he asked.

"I am afraid of Him in the night sometimes."

"You should love Him."

"I don't love much."

"Yes," he said. "You do . . . . When you love you wish to do things for. You wish to sacrifice for. You wish to serve."

"I don't love."

"You will. I know you will. Then you will be happy . . . . You cannot know about it unless you have it."

ERNEST HEMINGWAY, *A Farewell to Arms*

"The praise that comes of love," James M. Barrie remarked, "does not make us vain, but humble rather."

Is love possible? Every man knows that for himself. For me it is.

ERNEST HEMINGWAY

A devoted mother pleaded with her pastor to do all he could to help her alcoholic son. The pastor quickly became disgusted with the son, who was a repulsive fellow and not one bit cooperative, and gave up the mother's request as a hopeless task. The mother begged him to try again and put it like this: "If you cannot help him for his own sake, please do it for my sake. Remember, he's my son." There are people in the world so vicious and hateful that I cannot love them for themselves. There are folks in my town who are very hard to love. But when I have stood at the foot of Calvary and have heard the Saviour, who loved me enough to die for me, say to me as he points to every human being, "These are my children for whom I died; love them; preach the gospel to them; pray for them; help them in every possible way," why, that's an entirely different matter.

ARMIN C. OLDSEN

Thought, purpose, logic, industriousness, but without radiance or love: Isn't it an accurate description of Satan?

WILLIAM L. SULLIVAN

Love does not die easily. It is a living thing. It thrives in the face of all life's hazards, save one—neglect.

JAMES D. BRYDEN

John Frederick Oberlin, a Protestant pastor of a French village church, one morning rescued a Jewish peddler from a threatening mob. Taking him home, the minister placed him at the table with the rest of the family. That evening the Catholic priest came in for a chat, and the three of them—the Protestant minister, the Catholic priest, and the Jewish peddler—sat down before the fire. The mood of the evening was mellow, and the priest turned to the minister and said, "How I wish, my friend, that you and I were of the same religion!" The minister was silent a moment, and then, putting one arm around the Catholic and the other around the Jew, he said, "Those who love are of the same religion."

RUSSELL J. CLINCHY

Who loves the rain
And loves his home,
And looks on life with quiet eyes,
Him will I follow through the storm;
And at his hearth-fire keep me warm;
Nor hell nor heaven shall that soul surprise,
Who loves the rain,
And loves his home,
And looks on life with quiet eyes.

FRANCES WELLS SHAW

Love makes a difference. John was the busiest youth in the neighborhood. He was active in church, in Sunday school, in the scout troop. He carried papers and played in the high-school band. He didn't have time or money or energy for anything else. But then Alice moved into the neighborhood. Soon he was waiting to see her pass and hoping that she might smile. He found time to walk with her to the drugstore for a coke and to visit her home. John, who hadn't time or money or energy for any other activity, somehow found time to be with Alice. Love had made the difference. When people really love Jesus Christ, they somehow find time and money and energy for him. Genuine love finds a way.

DALE S. BRINGMAN

Infantile love follows the principle: "I love because I am loved." Mature love follows the principle: "I am

loved because I love." Immature love says: "I love you
because I need you." Mature love says: "I need you
because I love you."

ERICH FROMM, The Art of Loving

From the moment one falls in love, one becomes
sweet in temper.

MARMONTEL

It would be rather nice to be certain of a God [said
Reginald]; not for myself, but for other people. "God
bless my darling Sylvia, and keep her safe." Well, I say
it now, and oh! God, I mean it with all my heart, and
it's the only prayer I ever want You to consider. No, it
isn't, here's another one. "May she always go on loving
me." O Lord, that doesn't end it: "May I always go on
loving her"—that's the important one. We can put
those two into one if You like: May we always go on
loving each other.

A. A. MILNE, Two People

I am told that near the village of Leamington, England, in a small churchyard there stands a tombstone
with this inscription:

HERE LIES A MISER WHO LIVED FOR HIMSELF,
AND CARED FOR NOTHING BUT GATHERING PELF,
NOW, WHERE HE IS, OR HOW HE FARES,
NOBODY KNOWS AND NOBODY CARES.

Set that inscription over against this one on a plain
sarcophagus in Saint Paul's Cathedral, London:

SACRED TO THE MEMORY OF GENERAL CHARLES
GEORGE GORDON, WHO AT ALL TIMES AND EVERYWHERE

GAVE HIS STRENGTH TO THE WEAK, HIS SUBSTANCE TO
THE POOR, HIS SYMPATHY TO THE SUFFERING, HIS HEART
TO GOD.

FRANK FAGERBURG

Sir Ernest Shackleton, in describing the break for
safety which he and his companions made when they
were attempting to return from the expedition to the
South Pole, tells that he was profoundly impressed with
the things his companions considered important, as
contrasted with those which they threw away. The
money out of their pockets they put to one side. Even
food in their knapsacks they threw away. But the things
they did not leave were the pictures of loved ones and
letters from home. These they carried with them; and
in moments when it seemed as though the body needed
food, the soul would feed on the intangible inspirations
that come from love.

ALBERT W. BEAVER

"Uncle Hans," said Nathalie . . . "does love never
last?"

"Love can last if you get two people who are fine
enough. But they must both be fine, and the trouble is
that the right people so seldom meet. You see it sometimes. A man has had the luck to encounter a woman
who compels all the grand things in him—unselfishness, honour, gaiety, gladness . . . . But for the most part
people aren't patient enough, and they blame others for
their own failings."

HUGH WALPOLE, *Hans Frost*

Henry, in *Oldtown Folks*, says, "And my theology is,
once penetrate any human soul with the full belief that
God loves him, and you save him."

We like someone *because*. We love someone *although*.

HENRI DE MONTHERLANT

The greatest happiness of life is the conviction that we are loved, loved for ourselves, or rather loved in spite of ourselves.

VICTOR HUGO

Persons are to be loved; things are to be used.

REUEL HOWE

Gilbert Frankau in his story "Peter Jackson" describes the experiences of a man who fell in love with his own wife.

In a western town lived a preacher whose son grew up tall and straight, with a mind keen and clean and wholesome. In that same town lived a foul-mouthed, atheistic, and very brilliant doctor. A strong friendship grew up between the two. The doctor, with his brilliant mind, became a hero to the boy, and gradually there came an estrangement in the preacher's home. Under the father's roof the boy was irritable and unmanageable, contemptuous of his father's faith, resentful of even his mother's kindly concern. And whenever the interest of his father came into conflict with the interest of his friend, the boy consistently chose the latter's way and soon came almost completely under the spell of his atheistic hero, so much so that the people of the church shook their heads sadly and said, "He is getting more like the doctor than like his father. He is more the doctor's son than the son of his own father."

One midnight, the preacher, with heavy heart, stole softly into the bedroom of his son, to find the air filled with the fumes of alcohol, and the boy's mother kneeling by his bed, stroking his hair, kissing his forehead, caressing him. Looking up through the veil of tears, she said, "He won't let me love him when he's awake."

J. WALLACE HAMILTON,
Horns and Halos in Human Nature

He knew . . . what the old man was thinking as his tears flowed, and he, Rieux, thought it too: that a loveless world is a dead world, and always there comes an hour when one is weary of prisons, of one's work, and of devotion to duty, and all one craves for is a loved face, the warmth and wonder of a loving heart.

ALBERT CAMUS, *The Plague*

When General Robert E. Lee found an officer under his command gazing with satisfaction in the mirror, the general said, "Sir, you must be the happiest man in the world." "Why?" questioned the officer. "Because," said Lee, "you are in love with yourself, and you haven't a rival in the whole world."

There is an old tradition that the Apostle John lived the longest of all the apostles and that the brethren of the early church would again and again urge the old man to speak. He had known Jesus in the flesh, and he was the last of those who had. But the old, old man refused to say anything more than, "Little children, love one another." Over and over they urged him to tell them more about the Master and His spirit and His teaching. Finally he said, "Little children, love one another. There is nothing more." This is the gospel, and he that preaches another let him be anathema.

EDMUND B. CHAFFEE

I read recently of a boy who applied for a job as an usher in a theater, and the manager asked him, "What would you do in case of a fire?" "Oh, don't worry about me," said the boy, "I'd get out all right." Well, that self is in all of us. But not so long since I read about a boy in Korea, who was given the Congressional Medal posthumously. Once when he was ambushed he exposed himself and drew the fire of the enemy so that his buddies would escape, and that self, too, is in all of us. One self asks, "What is there in it for me? Nobody, nothing matters, just so my own self-centered, self-seeking wishes are satisfied." And the other self says, "Greater love hath no man than this, that a man lay down his life for his friend."

HAROLD COOKE PHILLIPS

A little girl sat in her rocking chair hugging a beautiful doll. She alternately kissed the doll, fondled it, and spoke words of endearment. Occasionally she glanced at her mother working at a desk on the other side of the room. As soon as she put down her pen, the child ran to her, climbed on her lap, and said: "I'm so glad you're through—I wanted to love you so much." "Did you, darling?" the mother asked. "I'm so glad; but I thought you were having a good time with your doll." "I was, Mommie," the little girl explained, "but I get tired of loving her because she never loves me back."

GWYNN MCLENDON DAY

Children need love, especially when they do not deserve it.

HAROLD S. HULBERT

8

First Book of Corinthians, Chapter Thirteen

1   Though I speak with the tongues of men and of angels, and have not charity, I am become as sounding brass, or a tinkling cymbal.

2   And though I have the gift of prophecy, and understand all mysteries, and all knowledge; and though I have all faith, so that I could remove mountains, and have not charity, I am nothing.

3   And though I bestow all my goods to feed the poor, and though I give my body to be burned, and have not charity, it profiteth me nothing.

4   Charity suffereth long, and is kind; charity envieth not; charity vaunteth not itself, is not puffed up,

5   Doth not behave itself unseemly, seeketh not her own, is not easily provoked, thinketh no evil;

6   Rejoiceth not in iniquity, but rejoiceth in the truth;

7   Beareth all things, believeth all things, hopeth all things, endureth all things.

8   Charity never faileth: but whether there be prophecies, they shall fail; whether there be tongues, they shall cease; whether there be knowledge, it shall vanish away.

9   For we know in part, and we prophesy in part.

10   But when that which is perfect is come, then that which is in part shall be done away.

11   When I was a child, I spake as a child, I understood as a child, I thought as a child: but when I became a man, I put away childish things.

12   For now we see through a glass, darkly; but then face to face: now I know in part; but then shall I know even as also I am known.

13   And now abideth faith, hope, charity, these three; but the greatest of these is charity.

The King James Version of the Holy Bible.

If I can speak with the tongues of men and of angels, but am destitute of Love, I have but become a loud-sounding trumpet or a clanging cymbal. If I possess the gift of prophecy and am versed in all mysteries and all knowledge, and have such absolute faith that I can remove mountains, but am destitute of Love, I am nothing. And if I distribute all my possessions to the poor, and give up my body to be burned, but am destitute of Love, it profits me nothing.

Love is patient and kind. Love knows neither envy nor jealousy. Love is not forward and self-assertive, nor boastful and conceited. She does not behave unbecomingly, nor seek to aggrandize herself, nor blaze out in passionate anger, nor brood over wrongs. She finds no pleasure in injustice done to others, but joyfully sides with the truth. She knows how to be silent. She is full of trust, full of hope, full of patient endurance.

Love never fails. But if there are prophecies, they will be done away with; if there are languages, they will cease; if there is knowledge, it will be brought to an end. For our knowledge is imperfect, and so is our prophesying; but when the perfect state of things is come, all that is imperfect will be brought to an end. When I was a child, I talked like a child, felt like a child, reasoned like a child: when I became a man, I put from me childish ways. For the present we see things as if in a mirror, and are puzzled; but then we shall see them face to face. For the present the knowledge I gain is imperfect; but then I shall know fully, even as I am fully known. And so there remain Faith, Hope, Love—these three; and of these the greatest is Love.

R. F. Weymouth, **The New Testament in Modern Speech.** James Clark & Co. Ltd. Cambridge, England. Used by permission.

13 I may speak with the tongues of man and of angels, but if
  I have no love,
   I am a noisy gong or a clanging cymbal;

2 I may prophesy, fathom all mysteries and secret lore,
 I may have such absolute faith that I can move hills from
   their place,
  but if I have no love,
   I count for nothing;

3 I may distribute all I possess in charity,
 I may give up my body to be burnt,
  but if I have no love,
   I make nothing of it.

4 Love is very patient, very kind. Love knows no jealousy;
5 love makes no parade, gives itself no airs, is never rude,
6 never selfish, never irritated, never resentful; love is never
 glad when others go wrong, love is gladdened by goodness,
7 always slow to expose, always eager to believe the best,
8 always hopeful, always patient. Love never disappears. As
 for prophesying, it will be superseded; as for 'tongues,'
 they will cease; as for knowledge, it will be superseded.
9 For we only know bit by bit, and we only prophesy bit
 by bit;
10 but when the perfect comes, the imperfect will be superseded.
11 When I was a child, I talked like a child, I thought like
 a child, I argued like a child; now that I am a man, I am
 done with childish ways.
12 At present we only see the baffling reflections in a mirror,
  but then it will be face to face;
 at present I am learning bit by bit,
  but then I shall understand, as all along I have
  myself been understood.

13 Thus 'faith and hope and love last on, these three,' but
 the greatest of all is love.

13. IF I speke with tungis of men and of aungels, and I haue not charite, I am made as bras sownynge or a cymbal tinkynge, ² and if I haue profecie, and knowe alle mysteries, and al kynnynge, and if I haue al feith so that I meue hillis fro her place and I haue not charite I am nou;t, ³ and if I departe alle my godis in to metis of pore men, and if I bitake my bodi so that I brenne, and I haue not charite it profetith to me no thing, ⁴ charite is pacient, it is benyngne,

charite enuyeth not, it doth not wickidli it is not blown ⁵ it is not coueitous, it sekith not tho thingis that ben his owne, it is not stired to wrathe, it thenkith not yuel, ⁶ it ioieth not on wickidnesse, but it ioieth to gidre to truthe, ⁷ it suffrith alle thingis: it bileueth alle thingis, It hopith alle thingis it susteyneth alle thingis, ⁸ charite fallith neuer doun, whether profecies schuln be voidid, ether langagis schulen ceese: ether science schal be distried,

⁹ for aparti we knowen and aparti we profecien, ¹⁰ but whanne that schal come that is perfi;t, that thing that is of parti schal be avoidid, ¹¹ whanne I was a litil child I spake as a litil child I vndirstood as a litil child, I thou;t as a litil child, but whanne I was made a man I voidid tho thingis that weren of a litil child, ¹² and we seen now bi a myrrour in derknesse: but thanne face to face, now I knowe of parti, but thanne I schal knowe as I am knowen, ¹³ and now dwellen feith hope & charite, these thre : but the moost of thes is charite.

Wyclif—1380, "The English Hexapla." By permission of Samuel Bagster & Sons Ltd. London.

I go on to show you a way beyond all comparison the best.

If I speak in the 'tongues' of men—aye, and of angels, too—but am without Love, I have become mere echoing brass, or a clanging cymbal! Even if I have the 'prophetic' gift and know all secret truths and possess all knowledge, or even if I have such perfect faith as to be able to move mountains, but am without Love, I am nothing! If I give all I possess to feed the hungry, and even if (to say what is boastful) I sacrifice my body, but am without Love, I am none the better! Love is long-suffering and kind. Love is never envious, never boastful, never conceited, never behaves unbecomingly. She is not self-seeking, not easily provoked, nor does she reckon up her wrongs. She has no sympathy with deceit, but has full sympathy with truth. She is proof against all things, always trustful, always hopeful, always patient. Love never dies. Are there 'prophetic' gifts?—they will be cast aside. Are there 'tongues'?—they will cease. Is there knowledge?—it will be cast aside. Our knowledge is incomplete, and our prophesying incomplete, but as soon as Perfection has come, what is incomplete will be cast aside. When I was a child, I talked like a child, thought like a child, reasoned like a child; now that I am a man, I have cast childish ways aside. As yet we see things dimly, reflected in a mirror, but then—face to face! As yet my knowledge is incomplete, but then it will be as full as God's knowledge of me is now. So then Faith, Hope, and Love last on—only these three—and of them the greatest is Love.

13
2
3
4
5
6
7
8
9
10
11
12
13

The Twentieth Century NEW TESTAMENT, Fleming H. Revell Company, Old Tappan, N.J.

Though I speak with 13
the tongues of men and of angels, and have not love,
I am become as sounding brass, or a tinkling cymbal.
And though I have the gift of prophecy, and under- 2
stand all mysteries and all knowledge, and though I
have all faith, so as to remove mountains, and have not
love, I am nothing. And though I give all my goods to 3
feed the poor, and deliver up my body to be burned,
and have not love, it profiteth me nothing. Love 4
suffereth long and is kind; love envieth not; love acteth 5
not rashly, is not puffed up; Doth not behave indecently, seeketh not her own, is not . . . provoked,
thinketh no evil; Rejoiceth not in iniquity, but re- 6
joiceth in the truth: Covereth all things, believeth all 7
things, hopeth all things, endureth all things. Love 8
never faileth: but whether there be prophecies, they
shall fail; whether there be tongues, they shall cease;
whether there be knowledge, it shall vanish away. 9
For we know in part, and we prophesy in part. And 10
when that which is perfect is come, then that which is
in part shall vanish away. When I was a child I talked 11
as a child; I understood as a child, I reasoned as a child;
but when I became a man, I put away childish things. 12
And now we see by means of a glass obscurely; but then
face to face: now I know in part, but then I shall know,
even as also I am known. And now abide these three, 13
faith, hope, love; but the greatest of these is love.

Ella C. Cell, "John Wesley's New Testament." Used by permission of Holt, Rinehart and Winston, Inc.

13 I may speak with the *tongues of men and of angels, yet if I have not love, I am a noisy gong or a sounding *cymbal. 2I may have the gift of *prophecy and understand all secrets and all knowledge, and I may have all faith so as to move mountains, yet if I have not love, I am nothing. 3I may give away all I have to the poor; and I may give my body to be burnt, yet if I have not love, I gain by it nothing.

4Love is patient and kind; love does not envy; love has no loud words in her mouth, no swelling thoughts in her heart; 5is not rude nor self-seeking nor easily angry; does not count up her wrongs; 6finds no pleasure in evil done to others, but delights in goodness. 7Love always forgives, always believes, always hopes, always bears patiently. 8Love never dies; but as for prophecy it will come to an end; as for tongues they will cease; as for knowledge it will come to an end. 9For we know in part, and we prophesy in part, 10but when that which is complete has come, then that which is in part shall come to an end.

11When I was a child I spoke like a child, I felt like a child, I thought like a child. But when I became a man, I put away childish things. 12For now we see only dark shapes in a looking-glass; but then face to face. Now I know in part, but then I shall know as fully as I am known. 13So, then, faith and hope and love remain, these three; but the greatest of them is love.

Charles Kingsley Williams, "The New Testament—A New Translation in Plain English," S•P•C•K• and Longmans. Green and Co., London, 1952. By kind permission of the Society for Promoting Christian Knowledge.

1   Though I should speak in the tongues of men and of angels, yet if I have not love, I have become

2   sounding brass or a tinkling cymbal. And though I should have the gift of prophecy, and know all mysteries and all knowledge; and though I should have all faith so as to remove mountains; yet if I

3   have not love, I am nothing. And though I should bestow all my goods to feed the poor, and though I should give up my body to be burnt, yet if I have not love, it profiteth me nothing.

4   Love is long-suffering, is kind; love envieth not;

5   love is not puffed up, vaunteth not itself, doth not behave unseemly, seeketh not its own, is not pro-

6   voked, beareth no malice; rejoiceth not over unrighteousness, but rejoiceth with the truth;

7   beareth all things, believeth all things, hopeth all things, endureth all things.

8   Love never faileth; but be there prophecies, they will be done away.

9   For we know in part, and we prophesy in part.

10 But when that which is perfect has come, that which

11 is in part will be done away. When I was a child I spoke as a child, I thought as a child, I reasoned as a child; now that I have become a man, I have

12 done away with the things of the child. For now we see by a mirror, in a riddle, but then face to face; now I know in part, but then I shall know, even as

13 I was known. But, even so, there abideth faith, hope, love, these three; but the greatest of these is love.

E. E. Cunnington, The New Testament of our Lord and Saviour Jesus Christ. Marshall, Morgan, & Scott Ltd. London. Out of print.

13   If I have all the eloquence of men or of angels, but   1
speak without love, I am simply a gong booming or a
cymbal clashing. If I have the gift of prophecy, under-   2
standing all the mysteries there are, and knowing everything, and if I have faith in all its fulness, to move
mountains, but without love, then I am nothing at all.
If I give away all that I possess, piece by piece, and if   3
I even let them take my body to burn it, but am without love, it will do me no good whatever.

Love is always patient and kind; it is never jealous;   4
love is never boastful or conceited; it is never rude or   5
selfish; it does not take offence, and is not resentful.
Love takes no pleasure in other people's sins but de-   6
lights in the truth; it is always ready to excuse, to   7
trust, to hope, and to endure whatever comes.

Love does not come to an end. But if there are   8
gifts of prophecy, the time will come when they must
fail; or the gift of languages, it will not continue for
ever; and knowledge—for this, too, the time will come
when it must fail. For our knowledge is imperfect and   9
our prophesying is imperfect; but once perfection
comes, all imperfect things will disappear. When I was   10
a child, I used to talk like a child, and think like a   11
child, and argue like a child, but now I am a man, all
childish ways are put behind me. Now we are seeing   12
a dim reflection in a mirror; but then we shall be seeing
face to face. The knowledge that I have now is imperfect; but then I shall know as fully as I am known.

In short, there are three things that last: faith, hope   13
and love; and the greatest of these is love.

13. THOUGH I spake with the tonges of men and angels, and yet had no love, I were even as soundinge brasse: or as a tynklynge Cymball. ²And though I coulde prophesy, and vnderstode all secretes, and all knowledge: yee, yf I had all fayth so that I coulde move mountayns oute of ther places, and yet had no love, I were nothynge. ³And though I bestowed all my gooddes to fede the poore, and though I gave my body even that I burned, and yet had no love, it profeteth me nothinge.

⁴Love suffreth longe, and is corteous. Love envieth not. Love doth not frowardly, swelleth not ⁵dealeth not dishonestly, seketh not her awne, is not provoked to anger, thynketh not evyll, ⁶reioyseth not in iniquite: but reioyseth in the trueth, ⁷suffreth all thynge, beleveth all thynges, hopeth all thynges, endureth in all thynges. ⁸Though that prophesyinge fayle, other tonges shall cease, or knowledge vanysshe awaye, yet love falleth never awaye.

⁹For oure knowledge is vnparfect, and oure prophesyinge is vnparfect. ¹⁰But when that which is parfect is come, then that which in vnparfect shall be done awaye.

¹¹When I was a chylde, I spake as a chylde, I vnderstode as a chylde, I ymagened as a chylde. But assone as I was a man, I put awaye childesshnes.

¹²Now we se in a glasse even in a darke speakynge: but then sall we se face to face. Now I knowe vnparfectly: but then shall I knowe even as I am knowen. ¹³Now abideth fayth, hope, and love, even these thre: but the chefe of these is love.

Tyndale—1534, "The English Hexapla." By permission of Samuel Bagster & Sons, Ltd. London.

1   Though I speak with the tongues of men and of angels, and have not love in my heart, I am become as sounding brass or a tinkling cymbal.

2   And though I have the gift of prophecy, and understand all mysteries and all knowledge; and though I have all faith, so that I could remove mountains, and have not love in my heart, I am nothing.

3   And though I bestow all my goods to feed the poor, and though I give my body to be burned, and have not love in my heart, I gain nothing.

4   Love is long-suffering and kind; love does not envy; love does not make a vain display of itself, and does not boast,

5   Does not behave itself unseemly, seeks not its own, is not easily provoked, thinks no evil;

6   Rejoices not over iniquity, but rejoices in the truth;

7   Bears all things, believes all things, hopes all things, endures all things.

8   Love never fails; but whether there be prophecies, they shall fail; whether there be tongues, they shall cease; whether there be knowledge, it shall vanish away.

9   For we know in part and we prophesy in part.

10   But when that which is perfect is come, then that which is imperfect shall come to an end.

11   When I was a child, I spoke as a child, I understood as a child, I thought as a child; but when I became a man, I put away childish things.

12   For now we see through a mirror, darkly; but then face to face. Now I know in part; but then shall I know even as also I am known.

13   And now abide faith, hope, love, these three; but the greatest of these is love.

The Holy Bible From Ancient Eastern Manuscripts, by George M. Lamsa; published by the A. J. Holman Company, Philadelphia, Pa.

13 I may be able to speak the languages of men and even of angels, but if I have not love, my speech is no more than a noisy gong or a clanging bell. ²I may have the gift of inspired preaching; I may have all knowledge and understand all secrets; I may have all the faith needed to move mountains—but if I have not love, I am nothing. ³I may give away everything I have, and even give up my body to be burned—but if I have not love, it does me no good.

⁴Love is patient and kind; love is not jealous, or conceited, or proud; ⁵love is not ill-mannered, or selfish, or irritable; love does not keep a record of wrongs; ⁶love is not happy with evil, but is happy with the truth. ⁷Love never gives up: its faith, hope, and patience never fail.

⁸Love is eternal. There are inspired messages, but they are temporary; there are gifts of speaking, but they will cease; there is knowledge, but it will pass. ⁹For our gifts of knowledge and of inspired messages are only partial; ¹⁰but when what is perfect comes, then what is partial disappears.

¹¹When I was a child, my speech, feelings, and thinking were all those of a child; now that I am a man, I have no more use for childish ways. ¹²What we see now is like the dim image in a mirror; then we shall see face to face. What I know now is only partial; then it will be complete, as complete as God's knowledge of me.

¹³Meanwhile these three remain: faith, hope, and love; and the greatest of these is love.

13   Though I speak with the tongues of men and of angels, and have not [love], I am become as sounding [bronze], or a tinkling cymbal.

2   And though I have the gift of prophecy, and understand all mysteries, and all knowledge; and though I have all faith so that I could remove mountains, and have not [love], I am nothing.

3   And though I bestow all my goods to feed the poor, and though I give my body to be burned, and have not [love], it profiteth me nothing.

4   [Love] suffereth long, and is kind; [love] envieth not; [love] vaunteth not itself, is not puffed up,

5   Doth not behave itself unseemly, seeketh not its own, is not easily provoked, thinketh no evil,

6   Rejoiceth not in iniquity, but rejoiceth in the truth;

7   Beareth all things, believeth all things, hopeth all things, endureth all things.

8   [Love] never faileth; but whether there be prophecies, they shall [be done away]; whether there be tongues, they shall cease; whether there be knowledge, it shall vanish away.

9   For we know in part, and we prophesy in part.

10   But when that which is perfect is come, then that which is in part shall be done away.

11   When I was a child, I spoke as a child, I understood as a child, I thought as a child; but when I became a man, I put away childish things.

12   For now we see [in a mirror], darkly; but then, face to face; now I know in part, but then shall I know even as also I am known.

13   And now abideth faith, hope, [love], these three; but the greatest of these is [love].

XIII.   ¹If with the tongues of men and of messengers I speak, and have not love, I have become brass sounding, or a cymbal tinkling; ²and if I have prophecy, and know all the secrets, and all the knowledge, and if I have all the faith, so as to remove mountains, and have not love, I am nothing; ³and if I give away to feed others all my goods, and if I give up my body that I may be burned, and have not love, I am profited nothing.

⁴The love is long-suffering, it is kind, the love doth not envy, the love doth not vaunt itself, is not puffed up, ⁵doth not act unseemly, doth not seek its own things, is not provoked, doth not impute evil, ⁶rejoiceth not over the unrighteousness, and rejoiceth with the truth; ⁷all things it beareth, all it believeth, all it hopeth, all it endureth.

⁸The love doth never fail; and whether there be prophecies, they shall become useless; whether tongues, they shall cease; whether knowledge, it shall become useless; ⁹for in part we know, and in part we prophesy; ¹⁰and when that which is perfect may come, then that which is in part shall become useless.

¹¹When I was a babe, as a babe I was speaking, as a babe I was thinking, as a babe I was reasoning, and when I have become a man, I have made useless the things of the babe; ¹²for we see now through a mirror obscurely, and then face to face; now I know in part, and then I shall fully know, as also I was known; ¹³and now there doth remain faith, hope, love—these three; and the greatest of these is love.

Literal Translation of the Holy Bible, Robert Young. Baker Book House, Grand Rapids, Michigan, 1953.

13 If I speak in the tongues of men and of angels, but have not
    love, I am a noisy gong or a clanging cymbal. 2And if I have
    prophetic powers, and understand all mysteries and all knowl-
    edge, and if I have all faith, so as to remove mountains, but
    have not love, I am nothing. 3If I give away all I have, and
    if I deliver my body to be burned, but have not love, I gain
    nothing.

    4Love is patient and kind; love is not jealous or boastful; 5it
    is not arrogant or rude. Love does not insist on its own way;
    it is not irritable or resentful; 6it does not rejoice at wrong, but
    rejoices in the right. 7Love bears all things, hopes all things,
    endures all things.

    8Love never ends; as for prophecy, it will pass away; as for
    tongues, they will cease; as for knowledge, it will pass away.
    9For our knowledge is imperfect and our prophecy is imper-
    fect; 10but when the perfect comes, the imperfect will pass
    away. 11When I was a child, I spoke like a child, I thought
    like a child, I reasoned like a child; when I became a man, I
    gave up childish ways. 12For now we see in a mirror dimly,
    but then face to face. Now I know in part; then I shall
    understand fully, even as I have been fully understood. 13So
    faith, hope, love abide, these three; but the greatest of these
    is love.

1 If I speak in the tongues of men and of angels but do not have love, I have become a sounding piece of brass or a clashing cymbal.

2 And if I have the gift of prophesying and understand all the sacred secrets and all knowledge, and if I have all the faith so as to transplant mountains, but do not have love, I am nothing.

3 And if I give all my belongings to feed others, and if I hand over my body, that I may boast, but do not have love, I am not profited at all.

4 Love is long-suffering and obliging. Love is not jealous, it does not brag, does not get puffed up,

5 does not behave indecently, does not look for its own interests, does not become provoked. It does not keep account of the injury.

6 It does not rejoice over unrighteousness, but rejoices with the truth.

7 It bears all things, believes all things, hopes all things, endures all things.

8 Love never fails. But whether there are gifts of prophesying, they will be done away with; whether there are tongues, they will cease; whether there is knowledge, it will be done away with.

9 For we have partial knowledge and we prophesy partially;

10 but when that which is complete arrives, that which is partial will be done away with.

11 When I was a babe, I used to speak as a babe, to think as a babe, to reason as a babe; but now that I have become a man, I have done away with the traits of a babe.

12 For at present we see in hazy outline by means of a metal mirror, but then it will be face to face. At present I know partially, but then I shall know accurately even as I am accurately known.

13 Now, however, there remain faith, hope, love, these three, but the greatest of these is love.

New World Translation of the Holy Scriptures, published by the Watch Tower Bible and Tract Society of Pennsylvania.

Charity is to be Preferred Before all Other Gifts

If I speak with the tongues of men, and of angels, and have not charity, I am become as sounding brass, or a tinkling cymbal.

2 And if I should have prophecy and should know all mysteries, and all knowledge, and if I should have all faith, so that I could remove mountains, and have not charity, I am nothing.

3 And if I should distribute all my goods to feed the poor, and if I should deliver my body to be burned, and have not charity, it profiteth me nothing.

4 Charity is patient, is kind: charity envieth not, dealeth not perversely; is not puffed up;

5 Is not ambitious, seeketh not her own, is not provoked to anger, thinketh no evil;

6 Rejoiceth not in iniquity, but rejoiceth with the truth;

7 Beareth all things, believeth all things, hopeth all things, endureth all things.

8 Charity never faileth away: whether prophecies shall be made void, or tongues shall cease, or knowledge shall be destroyed.

9 For we know in part, and we prophesy in part.

10 But when that which is perfect is come, that which is in part shall be done away.

11 When I was a child, I spoke as a child, I understood as a child, I thought as a child. But, when I became a man, I put away the things of a child.

12 We see now through a glass in a dark manner; but then face to face. Now I know in part; but then I shall know even as I am known.

13 And now there remain faith, hope, and charity, these three: but the greatest of these is charity.

Douay Version of the Holy Bible.

If I [can] speak in the tongues of men and [even] of angels, but have not love [that reasoning, intentional. spiritual devotion such as is inspired by God s love for and in us], I am only a noisy gong or a clanging cymbal.

2   And if I have prophetic powers—that is, the gift of interpreting the divine will and purpose; and understand all the secret truths and mysteries and possess all knowledge, and if I have (sufficient) faith so that I can remove mountains, but have not love [God's love in me] I am nothing—a useless nobody.

3   Even if I dole out all that I have [to the poor in providing] food, and if I surrender my body to be burned [or in order that I may glory], but have not love [God's love in me], I gain nothing.

4   Love endures long and is patient and kind; love never is envious nor boils over with jealousy; is not boastful or vain-glorious, does not display itself haughtily.

5   It is not conceited—arrogant and inflated with pride; it is not rude (unmannerly), and does not act unbecomingly. Love [God's love in us] does not insist on its own rights or its own way, for it is not self-seeking; it is not touchy or fretful or resentful; it takes no account of the evil done to it—pays no attention to a suffered wrong.

6   It does not rejoice at injustice and unrighteousness, but rejoices when right and truth prevail.

7   Love bears up under anything and everything that comes, is ever ready to believe the best of every person, its hopes are fadeless under all circumstances and it endures everything [without weakening].

8   Love never fails—never fades out or becomes obsolete or comes to an end. As for prophecy [that is, the gift of interpreting the divine will and purpose], it will be fulfilled and pass away; as for tongues, they will be destroyed and cease; as for knowledge, it will pass away [that is, it will lose its value and be superseded by truth].

9   For our knowledge is fragmentary (incomplete and imperfect), and our prophecy (our teaching) is fragmentary (incomplete and imperfect).

10   But when the complete and perfect [total] comes, the incomplete and imperfect will vanish away—become antiquated, void and superseded.

11   When I was a child, I talked like a child, I thought like a child, I reasoned like a child; now that I have become a man, I am done with childish ways and have put them aside.

12   For now we are looking in a mirror that gives only a dim (blurred) reflection [of reality as in a riddle or enigma], but then [when perfection comes] we shall see in reality and face to face! Now I know in part (imperfectly); but then I shall know and understand fully and clearly, even in the same manner as I have been fully and clearly known and understood [by God].

13   And so faith, hope, love abide; [faith, conviction and belief respecting man's relation to God and divine things; hope, joyful and confident expectation of eternal salvation; love, true affection for God and man, growing out of God's love for and in us], these three, but the greatest of these is love.

13   A Poem on Love: Love Gives Quality to All
        Other Gifts; Love Achieves the Greatest
        Wonders; Love Endures Forever.

And yet I will show you a way that is better by far:

If I could speak the languages of men, of angels too,
And have no love,
I am only a rattling pan or a clashing cymbal.
If I should have the gift of prophecy,
And know all secret truths, and knowledge in its every form,
And have such perfect faith that I could move mountains,
But have no love, I am nothing.
If I should dole out everything I have for charity,
And give my body up to torture in mere boasting pride,
But have no love, I get from it no good at all.
Love is so patient and so kind;
Love never boils with jealousy;
It never boasts, is never puffed with pride;
It does not act with rudeness, or insist upon its rights;
It never gets provoked, it never harbors evil thoughts;
Is never glad when wrong is done,
But always glad when Truth prevails;
It bears up under anything,
It exercises faith in everything,
It keeps up hope in everything,
It gives us power to endure in anything.

Love never fails;
If there are prophecies, they will be set aside;
If now exist ecstatic speakings, they will cease;
If there is knowledge, it will soon be set aside,
For what we know is incomplete and what we prophesy is incom-
    plete.

But when perfection comes, what is imperfect will be set aside.
When I was a child, I talked like a child,
I thought like a child, I reasoned just like a child.
When I became a man, I laid aside my childish ways.
For now we see a dim reflection in a looking-glass,
But then we shall see face to face,
Now what I know is imperfect,
But then I shall know perfectly, as God knows me.
And so these three, faith, hope, and love, endure,
But the greatest of them is love.

13   Even though I speak in every human and angelic language and have no love, I am as noisy brass or a loud-sounding cymbal. [2]And although I have prophetic gift and see through every secret and through all that may be known, and have sufficient faith for the removal of mountains, but I have no love, I am useless. [3]And though I give all my belongings for nourishment (to the needy) and surrender my body to be burned, but I have no love, I am not in the least benefited.

[4]Love endures long and is kind; love is not jealous; love is not out for display; [5]it is not conceited or unmannerly; it is neither self-seeking nor irritable, nor does it take account of a suffered wrong. [6]It takes no pleasure in injustice, but it sides happily with truth. [7]It covers up everything, has unquenchable faith, hopes under all circumstances, endures without limit.

[8]Love never fades out. As for prophesyings, they shall be rendered useless; as for tongues, they shall cease; as for knowledge, it shall lose its meaning. [9]For our knowledge is fragmentary and so is our prophesying. [10]But when the perfect is come then the fragmentary becomes antiquated.

[11]When I was a child I talked as a child; I entertained child interests. I reasoned like a child; but on becoming a man I was through with childish ways. [12]For now we see indistinctly in a mirror; but then face to face. Now we know partly, but then we shall understand as completely as we are understood.

[13]There remain, then, faith, hope, love, these three; but the greatest of these is love.

1   If I speak with the tongues of men and of angels, but have not love, I have become sounding brass or a clanging cymbal.

2   And if I have the power of prophecy and understand all mysteries and all knowledge, and if I have all faith, so as to remove

3   mountains, but have not love, I am nothing. And if I distribute all that I have to feed the poor, and if I give my body to

4   be burned, but have not love, it profits me nothing. Love is long-suffering, love is kind, is not jealous, love does not boast,

5   is not conceited, does not behave unbecomingly, does not seek her own interest, is not irritable, does not count up her wrongs,

6   does not rejoice in wickedness, but rejoices with the truth,

7   excuses all things, believes all things, hopes all things, endures

8   all things. Love never fails; but if there are prophetic powers, they will become useless; if there are tongues, they will cease;

9   if there is knowledge, it will become useless. For we know in

10   part and we prophesy in part, but when the perfect comes

11   what is in part will become useless. When I was a child, I talked like a child, I thought like a child, I reasoned like a child. Since I have become a man, I have no use for childish

12   things. For as yet we are looking at puzzling reflections in a mirror, but then face to face. As Yet I know in part, but then

13   I shall know fully, as I have been fully known. But now faith, hope, love—these three—endure. And the greatest of these is love.

The Riverside New Testament, William G. Ballantine. Houghton Mifflin Company, 1934.

13   I may speak in tongues of men or of angels, but if I am without love, I am a sounding gong or a clanging cymbal. I may have the gift of prophecy, 2 and know every hidden truth; I may have faith strong enough to move mountains; but if I have no love, I am nothing. I may dole out all I possess, or even give my 3 body to be burnt, but if I have no love, I am none the better.

Love is patient; love is kind and envies no one. Love 4 is never boastful, nor conceited, nor rude; never 5 selfish, not quick to take offence. Love keeps no score 6 of wrongs; does not gloat over other men's sins, but delights in the truth. There is nothing love cannot 7 face; there is no limit to its faith, its hope, and its endurance.

Love will never come to an end. Are there prophets? 8 their work will be over. Are there tongues of ecstasy? they will cease. Is there knowledge? it will vanish 9 10 away; for our knowledge and our prophecy alike are partial, and the partial vanishes when wholeness comes. When I was a child, my speech, my outlook, and my 11 thoughts were all childish. When I grew up, I had finished with childish things. Now we see only puz- 12 zling reflections in a mirror, but then we shall see face to face. My knowledge now is partial; then it will be whole, like God's knowledge of me. In a word, there 13 are three things that last for ever: faith, hope, and love; but the greatest of them all is love.

The Greatest Spiritual Gift

All Worthless, Lacking Love

Though I speak in the tongues of men and of an- 1
gels, but have no love, I am become a clanging brass,
or a clashing cymbal. Though I have the gift of 2
prophecy and understand all mysteries and all knowledge, and have all faith, so that I could remove mountains, but have not love, I am nothing. And though I 3
sell all my goods to feed the poor, and though I give
my body to be burned, but have not love, it avails me
nothing.

A Portrait of Jesus

Love suffers long and is kind; love envies not; love 4
makes no parade, is not puffed up, is not rude, nor 5
selfish, nor easily provoked. Love bears no malice, 6
never rejoices over wrong-doing, but rejoices when the
truth rejoices. It knows how to be silent, it is trustful, 7
hopeful, patient, enduring. Love never fails; but 8
though there are prophecies, they will fail; though
there are tongues, they will cease; though there is
knowledge, it will be superseded. For our knowing is 9
imperfect, and our prophesying is imperfect; but 10
when the perfect is come, then the imperfect will be
done away. When I was a child I spoke like a child, felt 11
like a child, thought like a child; now that I am become
a man, I have done with childish things.

Things That Abide

For now we see as in a mirror, and are baffled, but 12
then face to face; now I know in fragments, but then
shall I understand even as I also have been understood.
Faith, Hope, Love endure—these three; but the great- 13
est of these is Love.

The New Testament in Modern English, Helen Barrett Montgomery. Used by permission of the American Baptist Board of Education and Publication.

Christian Love—The Highest and Best Gift

If I were to speak with the combined eloquence of men and angels I should stir men like a fanfare of trumpets or the crashing of cymbals, but unless I had love, I should do nothing more. If I had the gift of foretelling the future and had in my mind not only all human knowledge but the secrets of God, and if, in addition, I had that absolute faith which can move mountains, but had no love, I tell you I should amount to nothing at all. If I were to sell all my possessions to feed the hungry and, for my convictions, allowed my body to be burned, and yet had no love, I should achieve precisely nothing.

XIII 1

This love of which I speak is slow to lose patience—it looks for a way of being constructive. It is not possessive: it is neither anxious to impress nor does it cherish inflated ideas of its own importance.

Love has good manners and does not pursue selfish advantage. It is not touchy. It does not compile statistics of evil or gloat over the wickedness of other people. On the contrary, it is glad with all good men when Truth prevails.

Love knows no limit to its endurance, no end to its trust, no fading of its hope: it can outlast anything. It is, in fact, the one thing that still stands when all else has fallen.

All Gifts Beside Love Will be Superseded One Day

For if there are prophecies they will be fulfilled and done with, if there are "tongues" the need for them will disappear, if there is knowledge it will be swallowed up in truth. For our knowledge is always incomplete and our prophecy is always incomplete, and when the Complete comes, that is the end of the Incomplete.

XIII 9

When I was a little child I talked and felt and thought like a little child. Now that I am a man my childish speech and feeling and thought have no further significance for me.

At present all we see is the baffling reflection of reality; we are like men looking at a landscape in a small mirror. The time will come when we shall see reality whole and face to face! At present all I know is a little fraction of the truth, but the time will come when I shall know it as fully as God now knows me!

In this life we have three great lasting qualities—faith, hope and love. But the greatest of them is love.

The New Testament in Modern English, J.B. Phillips, Translator. (© The Macmillan Company 1947, 1957).

13   If I can speak the languages of men and even of angels, but have no love, I am only a noisy gong or a clashing cymbal. If I am inspired to preach and 2 know all the secret truths and possess all knowledge, and if I have such perfect faith that I can move mountains, but have no love, I am nothing. Even if I give 3 away everything I own, and give myself up, but do it in pride, not love, it does me no good. Love is patient and kind. Love is not envious or boastful. It does 4 5 not put on airs. It is not rude. It does not insist on its rights. It does not become angry. It is not resentful. 6 It is not happy over injustice, it is only happy with truth. It will bear anything, believe anything, hope for 7 anything, endure anything. Love will never die out. If 8 there is inspired preaching, it will pass away. If there 9 is ecstatic speaking, it will cease. If there is knowledge, it will pass away. For our knowledge is imperfect and our preaching is imperfect. But when perfection 10 comes, what is imperfect will pass away. When I was 11 a child, I talked like a child, I thought like a child, I reasoned like a child. When I became a man, I put aside my childish ways. For now we are looking at a 12 dim reflection in a mirror, but then we shall see face to face. Now my knowledge is imperfect, but then I shall know as fully as God knows me. So faith, hope, 13 and love endure. These are the great three, and the greatest of them is love.

Edgar J. Goodspeed. "The Bible—An American Translation," The University of Chicago Press, Chicago, Illinois, n.d.

1   If I make use of the tongues of men and of angels, and have not love, I am like sounding brass, or a loud-tongued bell.

2   And if I have a prophet's power, and have knowledge of all secret things; and if I have all faith, by which mountains may be moved from their place, but have not love, I am nothing.

3   And if I give all my goods to the poor, and if I give my body to be burned, but have not love, it is of no profit to me.

4   Love is never tired of waiting; love is kind; love has no envy; love has no high opinion of itself, love has no pride;

5   Love's ways are ever fair, it takes no thought for itself; it is not quickly made angry, it has no thought of evil;

6   It takes no pleasure in wrongdoing, but has joy in what is true;

7   Love has the power of undergoing all things, having faith in all things, hoping all things.

8   Though the prophet's word may come to an end, tongues come to nothing, and knowledge have no more value, love has no end.

9   For our knowledge is only in part, and the prophet's word gives only a part of what is true:

10   But when that which is complete is come, then that which is in part will be no longer necessary.

11   When I was a child, I made use of a child's language, I had a child's feelings and a child's thoughts: now that I am a man, I have put away the things of a child.

12   For now we see things in a glass, darkly; but then face to face: now my knowledge is in part; then it will be complete, even as God's knowledge of me.

13   But now we still have faith, hope, love, these three; and the greatest of these is love.

The New Testament in Basic English. Cambridge University Press, New York, and Evans Brothers, Ltd. 1941. Used by permission.

ITS NECESSITY AND MORAL BEAUTY

1 If I should speak the languages of men and of angels, but have no love, I am no more than a noisy gong and a clanging cymbal.

2 And if I should have the gift of inspired utterance, and have the key to all secrets, and master the whole range of knowledge, and if I should have absolute faith so as to be able to move mountains,

3 but have no love, I am nothing. And if I should distribute all I have bit by bit, and should yield my body to the flames, but have no love, it profits me nothing.

4 Love is long-suffering; love is kind, and is not envious; love does

5 not brag; it is not conceited; it is not ill-mannered; it is not self-

6 seeking; it is not irritable, it takes no note of injury; it is not glad

7 when injustice triumphs; it is glad when the truth prevails. Always it is ready to make allowances; always to trust; always to hope; always to be patient.

ITS EXCELLENCE AND PERMANENCE

8 Love will never end. If there are inspired utterances, they will become useless. If there are languages, they will be discarded. If

9 there is knowledge, it will become useless. For our knowledge is incomplete, and our utterances inspired by God are incomplete,

10 but when that which is perfect has come, what is incomplete will

11 be useless. When I was a little child, I spoke as a little child, I thought as a little child. Now that I am grown to manhood, I have

12 discarded as useless my childish ways. We see now by means of a mirror in a vague way, but then we shall see face to face. Now my knowledge is incomplete, but then I shall have complete knowledge,

13 even as God has complete knowledge of me. So, there abide faith, hope, and love, but the greatest of them is love.

The New Testament, James A. Kleist, S.J., and Joseph L. Lilly, C.M. (Copyright 1954, 1956 by the Bruce Publishing Company).

13　　　　If I speak with the tongues of men and of angels, but have not love, I am become sounding brass, or a clanging cymbal. And if I have the gift of prophecy, and know all mysteries and all knowledge; and if I have all faith, so as to remove mountains, but have not love, I am nothing. And if I bestow all my goods to feed the poor, and if I give my body to be burned, but have not love, it profiteth me nothing. 4 Love suffereth long, and is kind; love envieth not; love vaunteth not itself, is not puffed up, doth not behave itself unseemly, seeketh not its own, is not provoked, taketh not account of evil, rejoiceth not in unrighteousness, but rejoiceth with the truth; beareth all things, believeth all things, hopeth all things, endureth all things. Love never faileth; but whether there be 8 prophecies, they shall be done away; whether there be tongues, they shall cease; whether there be knowledge, it shall be done away. For we know in part, and we prophesy in part: but when that which is perfect is come, that which is in part shall be done away. When 11 I was a child, I spake as a child, I felt as a child, I thought as a child: now that I am become a man, I have put away childish things. For now we see in a mirror, darkly; but then face to face: now I know in part; but then shall I know even as also I have been known. But now abideth faith, hope, love, these three; and the greatest of these is love.

The Modern Reader's Bible by Richard G. Moulton. (Copyright 1920 by the Macmillan Company, renewed 1948 by the Macmillan Company).

13   IF I HAD the gift of being able to speak in other languages without learning them, and could speak in every language there is in all of heaven and earth, but didn't love others, I would only be making noise. ²If I had the gift of prophecy and knew all about what is going to happen in the future, knew everything about *everything*, but didn't love others, what good would it do? Even if I had the gift of faith so that I could speak to a mountain and make it move, I would still be worth nothing at all without love. ³If I gave everything I have to poor people, and if I were burned alive for preaching the Gospel but didn't love others, it would be of no value whatever.

⁴Love is very patient and kind, never jealous or envious, never boastful or proud, ⁵never haughty or selfish or rude. Love does not demand its own way. It is not irritable or touchy. It does not hold grudges and will hardly even notice when others do it wrong. ⁶It is never glad about injustice, but rejoices whenever truth wins out. ⁷If you love someone you will be loyal to him no matter what the cost. You will always believe in him, always expect the best of him, and always stand your ground in defending him.

⁸All the special gifts and powers from God will someday come to an end, but love goes on forever. Someday prophecy, and speaking in unknown languages, and special knowledge—these gifts will disappear. ⁹Now we know so little, even with our special gifts, and the preaching of those most gifted is still so poor. ¹⁰But when we have been made perfect and complete, then the need for these inadequate special gifts will come to an end, and they will disappear.

¹¹It's like this: when I was a child I spoke and thought and reasoned as a child does. But when I became a man my thoughts grew far beyond those of my childhood, and now I have put away the childish things. ¹²In the same way, we can see and understand only a little about God now, as if we were peering at his reflection in a poor mirror; but someday we are going to see him in his completeness, face to face. Now all that I know is hazy and blurred, but then I will see everything clearly, just as clearly as God sees into my heart right now.

¹³There are three things that remain—faith, hope, and love— and the greatest of these is love.

The Living Bible, Tyndale House Publishers, Wheaton, Illinois. Used by permission.

XIII.—Though I could speak with the tongues of men, and of angels, but have not love, I become as sounding brass, or a noisy cymbal. And though I have prophecy, and know all secrets, and all knowledge; and though I have all faith, so as to remove mountains, but have not love, I am nothing. And though I spend all my goods in feeding the poor, and though I deliver my body to be burned, but have not love, I am nothing profited. Love suffers long, and is kind. Love envies not. Love does not vaunt; is not puffed up; does not behave itself unbecomingly; does not seek its own things; is not exasperated; does not imagine evil; does not rejoice in iniquity, but greatly rejoices in the truth: covers all things, believes all things, hopes all things, endures all things. Love never fails: but, whether prophecies, they will be out of use: or foreign languages, they shall cease: or science, it shall be abolished. For we know only in part, and prophesy in part. But when perfection is come, then what is in part will be done away. When I was a child, I spoke as a child, I conceived as a child, I reasoned as a child. But when I became a man, I put away childish things. For now we see through a glass obscurely; but then, face to face: now, I know in part; but then, I shall fully know, even as I am fully known. And now abide faith, hope, love, these three: but the greatest of these is love.

Doctors George Campbell, James MacKnight and Philip Doddridge, "The Sacred Writings of the Apostles and Evangelists of Jesus Christ, The New Testament," Baker Book House, Grand Rapids, Michigan, 1951.

1   I may speak with every tongue that men and angels use; yet, if I lack charity, I am no better than echoing bronze, or the clash of

2   cymbals. I may have powers of prophecy, no secret hidden from me, no knowledge too deep for me; I may have utter faith, so that I can move mountains; yet if I lack charity, I count for nothing.

3   I may give away all that I have, to feed the poor; I may give myself up to be burnt at the stake; if I lack charity, it goes for nothing.

4   Charity is patient, is kind; charity feels no envy; charity is never

5   perverse or proud, never insolent; has no selfish aims, cannot be

6   provoked, does not brood over an injury; takes no pleasure in

7   wrongdoing, but rejoices at the victory of truth; sustains, be-

8   lieves, hopes, endures, to the last. The time will come when we shall outgrow prophecy, when speaking with tongues will come to an end, when knowledge will be swept away; we shall never have

9   finished with charity. Our knowledge, our prophecy, are only

10   glimpses of the truth; and these glimpses will be swept away

11   when the time of fulfillment comes. (Just so, when I was a child, I talked like a child, I had the intelligence, the thoughts of a child;

12   since I became a man, I have outgrown childish ways.) At present, we are looking at a confused reflection in a mirror; then, we shall see face to face; now, I have only glimpses of knowledge;

13   then, I shall recognize God as he has recognized me. Meanwhile, faith, hope and charity persist, all three; but the greatest of them all is charity.

The New Testament in the translation of Monsignor Ronald Knox, Copyright 1944, Sheed and Ward Inc., New York. With the kind permission of His Eminence the Cardinal Archbishop of Westminster.